Samsung
Gear® S2

for
dummies®

A Wiley Brand

Samsung Gear® S2

for dummies

A Wiley Brand

by Eric Butow

Author of *Google Glass For Dummies*

Samsung Gear® S2 For Dummies®

Published by: **John Wiley & Sons, Inc.,** 111 River Street, Hoboken, NJ 07030-5774, www.wiley.com

Copyright © 2016 by John Wiley & Sons, Inc., Hoboken, New Jersey

Media and software compilation copyright © 2016 by John Wiley & Sons, Inc. All rights reserved.

Published simultaneously in Canada

For general information on our other products and services, please contact our Customer Care Department within the U.S. at 877-762-2974, outside the U.S. at 317-572-3993, or fax 317-572-4002. For technical support, please visit https://hub.wiley.com/community/support/dummies.

Wiley publishes in a variety of print and electronic formats and by print-on-demand. Some material included with standard print versions of this book may not be included in e-books or in print-on-demand. If this book refers to media such as a CD or DVD that is not included in the version you purchased, you may download this material at http://booksupport.wiley.com. For more information about Wiley products, visit www.wiley.com.

Library of Congress Control Number: 2016944311

ISBN: 978-1-119-27998-3

ISBN 978-1-119-27999-0 (ebk); ISBN ePDF 978-1-119-28000-2 (ebk)

Manufactured in the United States of America

10 9 8 7 6 5 4 3 2 1

Contents at a Glance

Table of Contents

Introduction

Welcome to *Samsung Gear S2 For Dummies*, which is your guide to using the Gear S2 smartwatch in your everyday life.

You may have picked up this book because you've already purchased a Samsung Gear S2 (congratulations!) or you're thinking about buying the Gear S2 thanks to all the interest and great reviews from the computing media. Either way, this book offers a great way to learn about Samsung's cutting-edge wearable device.

About This Book

Chances are that you're brand new to wearable computing. You may have been interested in wearing a smartwatch, but up until the Gear S2, you haven't seen a smartwatch that has interested you. Or you may already have a Gear S2 but want to know everything there is to know about it.

This is why this book is a soup-to-nuts presentation of how to set up the Gear S2, use it with your Android smartphone, and find apps that you can download and use to get the most use and fun from your smartwatch.

Unlike other books that require you to read an entire chapter in one sitting to understand what's going on, you can open this book anywhere and read about the topic that interests you at the moment. That is, you can search the book for information you need, read the page that has your answers, and then get back to work (or play).

You may notice that there are sidebars stippled throughout the book and you may run into one or more on the page you're reading. I cover the different types of sidebars later in this introduction.

I also use some basic technical conventions in this book that you should know about so you aren't confused or surprised by them:

>> Bold text means that you're meant to type the text just as it appears in the book. The exception is when you're working through a step list: Because each step is bold, any text I tell you to type is not bold.

>> Web addresses appear in monofont. If you're reading a digital version of this book on a device connected to the Internet, you can click the web address to visit that website, like this: www.dummies.com.

>> At a few points in this book, you see command sequences that tell you how to perform tasks. Each command in the sequence is separated by a command arrow. Each step in the sequence from left to right tells you the step you should take before proceeding to the next step. For example, here's how to change screen brightness: Press the Home button and then choose Settings ⇨ Display ⇨ Brightness to increase or decrease the brightness level.

Within this book, you may note that some web addresses break across two lines of text. If you're reading this book in print and want to visit one of these web pages, simply key in the web address exactly as it's noted in the text, pretending as though the line break doesn't exist. If you're reading this as an ebook, you've got it easy: Just click the web address to be taken directly to the web page.

Foolish Assumptions

Alas, computing technology isn't sophisticated enough (or small enough) yet for the Gear S2 to do everything on its own. You need to use a smartphone running at least Android 5.0 (Lollipop) with your Gear S2, and by the time you read this, you may be able to use the Gear S2 with an iPhone as well.

Though this book tells you how to use the Samsung Gear Manager app on your smartphone to work with your Gear S2, this book doesn't tell you how to use your smartphone. You should be able to find many good books for your specific smartphone and the operating system the smartphone uses, including books from Wiley, the publisher of this book.

The Gear S2 may be the first piece of wearable technology you've ever owned, so this book dishes out information about how to use the Gear S2 in easily digestible chunks, enabling you to get answers to your questions fast and then get back to using your Gear S2 to receive calls, text messages, and email messages, monitor your health, and much more.

Icons Used in This Book

TIP

The Tip icon points out insights or helpful suggestions for making life with your Gear S2 easier.

REMEMBER

Remember icons draw your attention to some particular information to keep in mind.

TECHNICAL STUFF

The Technical Stuff icon marks information of a highly technical nature that you can normally skip over.

WARNING

The Warning icon tells you to watch out! It marks important information that may save you headaches, not to mention your data, when you use the Gear S2.

Beyond the Book

I offer some extra content that you won't find in this book. To find some tips and tricks for making life easier with the Gear S2, check out the this book's Cheat Sheet, which you can find by going to www.dummies.com and typing "Samsung Gear S2 For Dummies Cheat Sheet" into the Search box.

You may also find updates to this book, if I have any, at www.dummies.com/extras/gears2. Also keep in mind that Google continually updates the Gear S2 hardware and software, so you can keep your book up-to-date by checking for updates.

Where to Go from Here

This book is yours, so you can annotate and augment the text in any way you want — with a highlighter pen, by writing notes in the margins, or by placing bookmarks at several strategic locations throughout the book so that you can return to those places quickly.

If you've just purchased the Gear S2 and want to get grounded in what your new smartwatch is all about, flip to Chapter 1. But if you can't wait to get the Gear S2 out of the box and start playing with it, flip the pages to Chapter 2 so that you can set up the Gear S2, put it on your wrist, and start exploring your new smartwatch.

1

Getting to Know You, Gear S2

IN THIS PART . . .

Learning what the Samsung Gear S2 is and what you can do with it

Getting familiar with the Gear S2, including how to fit the smartwatch on your wrist properly

Finding out how to charge the Gear S2 when the battery runs low

Changing Gear S2 settings and the watch face

Setting up the Gear Manager app on your Android smartphone and using Gear Manager with your Gear S2

Chapter 1

Introducing Your Gear S2

Congratulations on your purchase of the Samsung Gear S2. How does it feel to be on the cutting edge?

The fact that you possess a Gear S2 means that you don't think smartwatches are a fad or just plain unnecessary. You know that the Gear S2 is an easy way for you to get information you need quickly, such as the time and place of your next appointment, by looking at the Gear S2 on your wrist instead of fumbling for the smartphone in your pocket.

In this chapter, I start by giving you a (very) brief history of smartwatch development. Next, you learn about how the Gear S2 fits into the larger ecosystem of connected devices better known as the Internet of Things. You also get an overview of the two Gear S2 models and how they compare.

Then I tell you about the issues involved with pairing your Gear S2 with your Android smartphone. Next, you get to know the Gear S2 apps that are preinstalled on the smartwatch. You also learn how to shop for Gear S2 accessories. Finally, this chapter shows you all the good stuff that's in your Gear S2 box.

Presenting a Brief History of Time . . . on Smartwatches

Smartwatches aren't a new phenomenon. In January 1946, newspaper readers first saw popular comic strip detective Dick Tracy use his new "wrist radio," and later a "wrist TV," to fight crime. (You remember newspapers: those large rectangular sheets of paper with writing on them.) You may have seen smartwatches used in such cartoons as *The Jetsons* and *Inspector Gadget* growing up.

What's more, Samsung was an early developer of watch phones with the bulky but still impressive looking SPH-WP10 watch phone the company introduced way back in 1999. (You can read more about this watch at http://www.phonearena. com/news/Did-you-know-that-Samsung-announced-a-watch-phone-in-1999_ id69376.) As with many early versions of hardware and software that later changed our lives, the 1999 Samsung smartwatch didn't click with consumers. (There's no word on how popular it was with secret agents.)

Today's kids don't have to read newspapers (not that they do, anyway) or watch cartoons to get an idea of what smartwatches are all about — nowadays, smartwatches really do exist and are maturing fast. I say maturing because despite the fact that there isn't a "killer app" as of this writing that would cause people to buy a smartwatch just for that app, today's smartwatches do useful things.

Modern smartwatches also look like watches — that is, they're either round or square in shape and are similar in thickness to what you find in analog or digital watches.

Connecting Thing 1 to Thing 2

Smartwatches have also benefited from the growth of a network of physical objects including devices, buildings, vehicles, appliances, and even clothes that can exchange data with one another. You may have heard the name of this network bandied about in the media: The Internet of Things, also known by its acronym IoT. Technology companies are working fast to connect all your devices together so that they can communicate with each other and (ostensibly) make our lives easier. It makes sense that you'll want to see messages from IoT devices both on your smartphone and by holding up your wrist and looking at your smartwatch.

Samsung is a conglomerate that produces a number of consumer electronics including TVs, refrigerators, and even washers and dryers. You see where I'm going: Samsung wants to give you not only the complete experience of pairing its Galaxy smartphones, Galaxy Tab tablets, and Gear smartwatches, but it also wants to use the Gear S2 to entice you to buy Samsung everything.

As part of this "Samsung, Samsung everywhere!" strategy, Samsung has taken a page out of Apple's playbook and decided to support its own smartwatch operating system . . . sort of. Samsung is a lead developer in the open-source Tizen operating system (OS) and uses Tizen in its TVs, in a few smartphone models, and, most important, on the Gear S2.

Getting to Know the Gear S2 Models

The Gear S2 comes in two models: the "standard" Gear S2, which is just called the Gear S2, and the Gear S2 Classic. Both models have many of the same features:

>> The watch itself is 1.2 inches in diameter and the screen resolution is 360 x 360 pixels. The watch case is made of stainless steel.

>> Both watches have a bezel, or a ring, around the watch face.

>> A 1.0 GHz dual-core processor powers the Gear S2.

>> The Gear S2 has 512MB of memory.

>> The watch possesses a maximum of 4GB of internal storage, but Samsung takes pains to note that the actual amount of memory you have available on the watch to store data is lower because the Gear S2 has the Tizen OS and important apps preinstalled.

>> Both models provide you with a 2.4GHz Wi-Fi connection that connects to 802.11 b/g/n/e standards.

>> You can connect to other devices using Bluetooth.

>> Both models have Near Field Communication (NFC) support so that you can connect with other devices within inches of each other. Samsung plans to use NFC with its Samsung Pay service so that you can use the Gear S2 to pay for stuff, with this feature becoming available sometime in 2016.

>> When you're ready to recharge your Gear S2, you use the charging dock that comes with your watch. (You learn more about your charging dock in Chapter 2, when you charge the Gear S2 for the first time.)

>> Both smartwatch models have the same version of the Tizen OS and the same apps preinstalled.

>> Last but not least, you can select from a variety of watch face designs so that when you see the time on your Gear S2, you'll be reminded about how cool your Gear S2 is.

So what are the differences between the two models? I'm glad you asked.

Meeting the plain ol' Gear S2

The "standard" Gear S2 has a more streamlined design with a plastic wrist strap that Samsung calls Elastomer as well as a flat bezel. The Gear S2 comes in only two colors: Silver and Dark Gray, as you can see in Figure 1-1.

Source: http://www.samsung.com/us/explore/gear-s2/?cid=ppc-

If you already purchased your Gear S2 at your favorite data carrier, such as Verizon or Sprint, you already know the kicker: You can purchase a 3G or 4G version of the Gear S2 so that you can make voice calls, text, send email, and receive notifications through your phone without a smartphone nearby.

As a result, the Gear S2 is a little heavier than its Classic counterpart because it contains a speaker, an electronic SIM card, and a 300mAh battery — 50mAh more than the Gear S2 Classic.

Fancying the Gear S2 Classic

The Gear S2 Classic is so named because the design of the watch evokes a more classic watch look. For example, the bezel has little serrated "teeth," which you also find on many standard watches. The Gear S2 Classic rounds out the classic look by sporting a leather wrist strap.

The Gear S2 Classic comes in three colors: black, platinum, and 18-karat rose gold. In addition to the slick black look, you can also purchase a black 3G version so that you can communicate with the Internet using your carrier's data network. (Sorry, there is no 4G version as of this writing.)

The platinum and rose-gold Gear S2 models, shown in Figure 1-2 along with the black model, come in Bluetooth only and will set you back another $100. The rose-gold model has an added benefit: You can impress others by telling them that the 18-karat rose gold gets its color through a combination of three metals: 75 percent gold, 21 percent copper, and 4 percent silver.

FIGURE 1-2:
The black, rose gold, and platinum Gear S2 Classic models.

Like the mystery of where your missing socks went after you p   them in the dryer, the Gear S2 Classic doesn't allow you to connect with th outside digital world through a data carrier's wireless network. Instead, you h   to use the Gear S2 Classic's Bluetooth connection to connect with your Andr   smartphone.

REMEMBER

You'll still be able to get notifications of voice calls, te   messages, and email messages on your Gear S2 Classic, but you'll have to pu   ut your smartphone to take your call or read your messages. This is why the G   S2 Classic has a 250mAh battery and is a little lighter than its "standard" Gea 2 counterpart.

Pairing Your Smartphone

So the Gear S2 hasn't quite reached the standards set by Dick Tracy's wrist radio/TV. That is, you can't use the Gear S2 by itself to get the most out of it — you need to use your Gear S2 with your Android smartphone. Samsung says Gear S2 supports most Android smartphones that run Android 4.4 (also known as KitKat) or later, and your phone needs to have at least 1.5GB of memory.

If you're unsure about whether the Gear S2 supports your phone, here's the short answer: If you have a Samsung smartphone running KitKat or later, you're good. You can do anything you want with your Gear S2, including sync your email between your phone's email account and your Gear S2, as well as share the Wi-Fi profile with your phone on your Gear S2. (If you're excited about Wi-Fi profile sharing, hold tight: I cover that topic in more detail in Chapter 4.)

If you don't own a Samsung smartphone, connecting your smartphone to your Gear S2 is a more interesting experience. For example, if you don't have a Samsung smartphone, you can't sync your email messages between your phone and your watch. Other features such as Wi-Fi profile sharing and receiving text messages may also be limited (or not work at all). If you're not sure whether you have these capabilities, you should pick up your smartphone and give Samsung a call at 1-800-SAMSUNG (that's 1-800-726-7864).

Getting to Know the Gear S2 Apps

Your Gear S2 comes with a number of preinstalled apps that enable you to do things on the smartwatch that you may find useful. Table 1-1 presents a list of preinstalled apps that you can use on your Gear S2:

TABLE 1-1   **Pre-Installed Gear S2 Apps**

Icon	App
	The Messages app allows you to view messages and then either type a reply or call the messenger back.
	The Phone app shows you notifications for incoming calls so that you can grab your smartphone and take the call (or not). The app also synchronizes the Contacts list on your smartphone so that you can initiate a call from the Contacts list or just tap the phone number on your watch. If you have the "standard" Gear S2 or the black Gear S2 classic supported by a data carrier, you'll also be able to respond and talk on your watch. Otherwise, you need to get out your smartphone to receive your call.

Icon	App
	S Health tracks your physical activity and measures your pulse while you move by using the sensors on the back of the Gear S2. You learn how to set up and use S Health in Chapter 9.
	The Nike+ Running app uses sensors on the back of the Gear S2 to monitor your vital signs as you run and keeps track of your statistics so that you can improve your running performance.
	The Settings app allows you to view and change Gear S2 settings, which you learn more about in Chapter 3.
	The Schedule app shows you your upcoming appointment as well as a brief note about your following appointment, if there is one.
	S Voice is the default voice command app that lets you tell your Gear S2 what to do. You learn how to make the Gear S2 obey your every command in Chapter 8.
	The Weather app shows you the current weather information for your location. You can also add another location and view the current conditions in that location.
	Alarm is what you expect: You can add an alarm so that your watch will make noise when the alarm is triggered. If you want to postpone the alarm for five minutes, you can activate the snooze option. You can also delete an alarm when you have no further use for it.
	Timer allows you to set the amount of time for the countdown, and when the timer reaches zero, the watch makes noise to let you know your time is up.
	Stopwatch lets you time an event. You can start the stopwatch, pause it, restart it, and stop it. You can also view a stopwatch log so that you can compare times from previous events.
	World Clock allows you to add one or more cities around the world and show the current time in the city or cities.
	Bloomberg shows you a summary of your stock portfolio and gives you a recap of the latest news from the business world.

(continued)

TABLE 1-1 *(continued)*

Icon	App
	CNN is a popular online news source (not so much on TV), and you can have CNN deliver up-to-the-minute news updates to your Gear S2.
	ESPN shows you a summary of the latest sports scores and news. You need to install the ESPN Companion for Gear app on your smartphone to use the ESPN app on your Gear S2.
	News Briefing is a news aggregator from Flipboard and provides you with a summary of the latest news. Swipe up and down on the screen to view leading news stories in a variety of categories.
	Music Player lets you control and play music not only on the Gear S2 but also on your smartphone.
	Samsung Milk Music is Samsung's streaming music service that you can use to play music on not only your Gear S2 but also your smartphone.
	Gallery allows you to view images you've captured on your Gear S2. You can capture an image by holding down the Home button and then swiping left or right on the screen.
	Buddy is an app that allows you to select your favorite contacts from your Contacts list. Within the Buddy app, you can tap your buddy to quickly call or send a message to that person.
	Email is a straightforward app: It synchronizes with the email accounts on your smartphone and then displays a brief summary of the email message on the screen. Tap the summary on the screen to read the entire message and reply to it by either speaking or typing your reply on the Gear S2.
	Find My Phone is a useful little app to find your phone. You open the app, tap Start, and then listen for your smartphone making noise. The smartphone screen turns on, too.
	Maps shows you your current location on a very small map. You can also search for a specific location and for businesses or features near you, such as the nearest lake, so that you can enjoy a day out.
	Voice Memo lets you record a voice memo on your Gear S2 that you can play back later. You can also save the voice memo as a text file to read.

Making Your Watch Yours

Samsung loves to provide you with options t̶o̶ ̶p̶e̶r̶s̶o̶n̶a̶l̶i̶z̶e̶ ̶y̶o̶u̶r̶ ̶d̶e̶v̶i̶c̶e̶s̶, including the Gear S2. A̶l̶l̶ ̶y̶o̶u̶ ̶n̶e̶e̶d̶ ̶t̶o̶ ̶d̶o̶ ̶i̶s̶ ̶v̶i̶s̶i̶t̶ the Gear S2 accessories website on your
c̶o̶m̶p̶u̶t̶e̶r̶ ̶o̶r̶ smartphone at http://www.samsung.com/us/mobile/wearable-
tech-accessories. The Wearable Tech Accessories page on the Samsung website
(see Figure 1-3) shows you a list of bands that you can purchase to replace your
current band.

FIGURE 1-3: Samsung has seven replacement bands to choose from.

Source: http://www.samsung.com/us/mobile/wearable-tech-accessories?filter=smartwatchbands

The Gear S2 model you have determines the watch straps you can purchase. If
you have a Gear S2 Classic, you can choose only a brown or gray leather band.
The other bands are for the plain old Gear S2. Granted, Samsung has pretty slim
pickings when it comes to bands, but plenty of other bands are available. Just type
Samsung watch bands into your favorite search engine and enjoy visiting online
stores just waiting to sell you watch straps.

Discovering What's in the Box (Hint: It's Not Jack)

If you're reading this book, chances are that you've received (or picked up) your
Gear S2 already and you've probably opened up the box with the excitement you

remember as a kid opening up a gift for yourself. But if you're reading this book wondering what you'll get in the box, or if you're waiting for my permission to open the box, keep reading! Here's what you find inside:

>> The watch itself, with the wrist strap attached.

>> A small bag that contains a smaller wrist strap in case the default wrist strap is too big. I tell you about swapping out the wrist strap in Chapter 2.

>> The charger that sits nicely on a desk or other flat surface. You learn about how to place the Gear S2 on the charger in Chapter 2.

>> The travel adapter, which is a black plug that you insert into a wall outlet or, preferably, a surge protector outlet.

>> A three-foot cable that connects your charger to the travel adapter. One end of the cable is a USB connector, which means that you can connect your charger to a computer and swap files. You find out more about that cool trick in Chapter 4.

>> Teeny, tiny printed books and brochures that provide some important information and a quick reference guide to the watch and with luck, you can read the tiny print.

Figure 1-4 contains a photo of all the stuff in the box that I received with my Gear S2 Classic.

FIGURE 1-4:
All the stuff
that comes in
the box.

Chapter 2

Taking the Time to Set Up Gear S2

Okay, you've taken everything out of the Gear S2 box. It's time to turn on the watch and start playing, right? Uh, no.

The Gear S2 battery isn't fully charged when you take it out of the box because the battery was tested before it was placed in the box. So the first thing you should do is check the watch and make sure that the device looks good. Remove the plastic adhesive coverings and look for scratches or any other outer signs of wear and tear that your brand-new device shouldn't have.

In this chapter, I start by reviewing the hardware features of the Gear S2. Next, you learn how to charge the Gear S2 to get the battery life up to 100 percent. Then you find out how to start up the Gear S2 and set up your smartwatch for the first time. Finally, I show you how to put the Gear S2 on your wrist and adjust it for optimum comfort. In case you don't like the large band, I show you how to swap out the large band for the smaller one that comes in the box.

If you do find there are scratches or any other defects in your Gear S2 or related components such as the charger, your Gear S2 is covered by a limited warranty. Call Samsung at 1-800-SAMSUNG (that's 1-800-726-7864) to talk to a real person about your problems, obtain a new Gear S2 or related components, and return the broken equipment to Samsung.

Inspecting the Gear S2 Hardware

With the plastic adhesive coverings taken off the watch, hold the smartwatch with the screen toward you. The smartwatch itself is called the case. You know that the watch is right side up when the smaller wrist strap (the one with the buckle) is above the smartwatch case and the larger strap (that's the strap with the adjustment holes) is below the case.

REMEMBER

By the way, I'm not going to leave you behind with a bunch of dense text. This chapter has plenty of photos that illustrate all the features, instructions, and other good stuff.

I start off with Figure 2-1, which shows the black Gear S2 Classic that I own. This model sports the serrated bezel that borders the watch face. (If you have the standard Gear S2, the bezel is smooth.) Confirm that the bezel moves as it should by placing your index finger and thumb on either side of the bezel and then moving the bezel left and right. If the bezel doesn't move in one or both directions, it's time to call Samsung.

Now turn the case so that you see the right side of the watch that you see in Figure 2-2. You see two buttons. The button on the top is the Back button: When you press it, you go back to the previous screen.

The bottom button is the one you press to turn the power on as well

FIGURE 2-1:
The bezel appears around the watch face with the smaller strap on top and the larger strap on the bottom.

FIGURE 2-2:
The Back button is on the top and the Power/ Home button is on the bottom.

as to return to the Home screen, which is the screen that shows you the clock with the current time.

When you turn on the watch, the back of the watch warms up because you own an electronic gadget. The back of the watch contains a pair of sensors that light up on the back of the watch when you have an app that wants to count your heart rate.

For example, if you have the Heart Wave watch face, you can tell this face to take your pulse. As the Gear S2 takes your pulse, the two heart rate sensor lights light up on the back of the watch. Figure 2-3 shows you what these two little sensor lights look like since you can't see the bottom of the watch when it's on your wrist.

Samsung recommends that you don't look at the sensor lights because you can hurt your eyes. If you do look at the lights to ensure that they work, look for just a second or two. Otherwise, I hope that the pain in your eyes and head will compel you to stop.

The charger is a curious thing: It's shaped roughly in the form of an L. The horizontal part of the L sits on your desk, and you charge the Gear S2 using the vertical bar. One side of the vertical bar, shown in Figure 2-4, is magnetized so that you can place the bottom of the watch against the bar. When you do, the Gear S2 starts charging. Hang tight; I get to charging shortly.

FIGURE 2-3: Two sensor lights appear on the back of the watch.

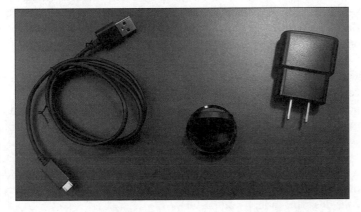

FIGURE 2-4: Here's a nice family portrait of the charger, cable, and plug.

Your smartphone plug and cable look a lot like the plug and cable you find with your smartphone, as you can see in Figure 2-4. The connector on one end of the cable is smaller than the connector on the other end. The small connector plugs into the port on the charger. The other connector is a USB connector, which means that if you're not close to your power plug, you can charge your Gear S2 by plugging the USB connector into another device, such as a laptop's USB port.

REMEMBER

If you plug your Gear S2 into a laptop or desktop computer to charge it, remember that the laptop or computer has to be on for the Gear S2 charger to receive power. Your Gear S2 may also take longer to charge from your computer because the power coming into your computer is powering your computer parts as well as your Gear S2 charger.

Charging Up Your Gear

Now that you've seen your Gear S2 and ensured that not only the smartwatch but also all the parts appear to be in good working order, you can charge your smartwatch. The good people at Samsung test your battery along with the rest of the Gear S2 before they send it off so that some lucky person like you can buy it, which means that the battery is drained.

Now breathe in and out a couple of times, because you have to perform one final test: Make sure that the Gear S2 can charge fully and hold a full charge. This will take a few minutes, so get some other work done . . . or even relax. (Do people actually do that anymore?)

Start by plugging the cable to the charger and to your plug. Then insert the plug into your wall outlet or, even better, a surge protector. (Insert your favorite trite safety slogan here.) Now, place the back of the watch against the vertical bar on the charger with the left side of the watch case (the one without buttons) resting on the bottom of the charger.

The vertical bar has two sides, and only one side is magnetized. So which side do you use? Samsung made it easy by putting its logo on the side of the bar that is not the side you use. You guessed right: The glass on the front of the case isn't magnetized, so you have to place the back of the case on the proper side of the vertical bar (see Figure 2-5).

If you don't believe me, put the front or back of the case on the side of the bar with the Samsung logo and watch your smartwatch fall off the charger and clatter on your desk (or table, if you prefer).

When you place the back of the Gear S2 on the correct side, notice the magnet on the back of the case pulling it to the vertical bar on the charger. When the case and the vertical bar make contact, move the charger around so that you can see the Gear S2 screen. You can see the battery strength percentage on the watch screen, which registers a range from 0 percent (empty) to 100 percent (full).

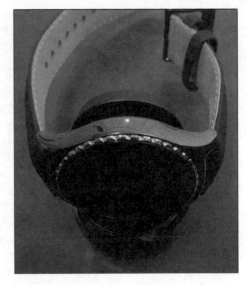

TIP

The screen automatically rotates on the charger so that you can see the percentage properly without having to remove the watch from the charger.

The Gear S2 screen turns off about 15 seconds after you connect it to the charger, but you don't need to turn the screen back on. Instead, look at the bottom of the charger below the front of the Gear S2 screen.

FIGURE 2-5:
The back of the Gear S2 connects to the magnetized side of the vertical bar.

At the bottom of the charger, you see a light when your watch is charging (see Figure 2-6). If the light is red, that means your battery isn't full and you should keep the Gear S2 connected to the charger. When the light is green, the battery is full and you can remove it from the charger.

FIGURE 2-6:
The light on the charger tells you whether you need to wait to fully charge your Gear S2.

After you release the Gear S2 from the charger, if you're viewing the smartwatch screen you see the battery strength percentage amount on the screen for a second or two. If the charger light is green, the percentage on the screen should be 100.

REMEMBER

The battery will last for about two to three days before you have to recharge your Gear S2. Just as with your smartphone, if you use one or more apps on your Gear S2 that require a lot of battery juice, your battery won't last as long. When your Gear S2 runs (or nearly runs) out of power, plan on doing something else with your time for about two hours as your smartwatch charges back up to 100 percent.

TIP

You can charge your Gear S2 while the smartwatch is on. However, charging may take longer because the battery is already using its power to keep the Gear S2 running. So if you don't expect to use your Gear S2 soon after you place the smartwatch on the charger, you charge it faster by turning off the Gear S2 and letting the battery focus on charging alone.

Starting and Setting Up the Gear S2

When the light on the charger turns green, you're finally (finally!) ready to start the Gear S2 for the first time. Hold down the Power button until you feel the watch vibrate; then release your finger. The Gear S2 logo appears on the screen, and you have to wait a few seconds more for the Tizen operating system to load. (I tell you more about the Gear S2's Tizen OS in Chapter 1.)

When the Gear S2 is finished starting up, you see the Welcome screen shown in Figure 2-7.

After you tap the screen, a message appears that asks you to install the Samsung Gear app on your smartphone, as shown in Figure 2-8. Yes, you need to use an Android smartphone with your Gear S2. Even if you purchased your Gear S2 from a phone carrier so that you can make calls on your carrier's network without a smartphone, you need to use the Gear Manager app on your smartphone to install apps on and manage your Gear S2.

FIGURE 2-7:
Welcome to your Gear S2.

As of this writing, Samsung has pre-installed Gear Manager on its latest Galaxy S7 Android smartphone. However, if you have an older Android smartphone, you need to install the Gear Manager app, as you learn to do shortly. There's also media chatter about a Gear Manager app for the iPhone as of this writing, so you may want to check the App Store on your iPhone to see whether the Gear Manager app is available now.

You can't do anything else on your Gear S2 after this point until Gear Manager is installed. The smartwatch screen turns off after 15 seconds.

FIGURE 2-8:
You can't do anything with your Gear S2 until you set up Gear Manager on your smartphone.

Installing the Gear Manager app on your smartphone

Now you need to turn on or awaken your Android smartphone, which in this example is my Samsung Galaxy S6. Open your Apps screen and then tap Galaxy Apps. You may need to swipe to the appropriate page within the Apps screen to find the Galaxy Apps icon. Then follow these steps to set up your smartphone to work with your Gear S2 watch:

1. **In the Galaxy Apps screen, tap Search in the upper-right corner of the screen.**

   The Search screen appears.

2. **Type** Samsung Gear **in the Search box.**

   Samsung Gear Manager appears at the top of the results list.

3. **Tap Samsung Gear Manager, shown in Figure 2-9.**

   The Samsung Gear Manager app appears at the top of the apps list that you see in Figure 2-10. The Download icon appears to the right of the Samsung Gear Manager entry. (You can read details about the app, if you want, by tapping its name in the list.)

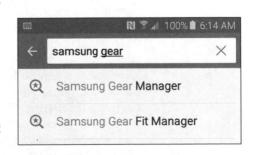

FIGURE 2-9:
The Samsung Gear Manager app is at the top of the list so that you can find it quickly.

4. **Tap the Download icon.**

As with most apps that you want to install on your smartphone, the Gear Manager app requires that you accept the terms of use before you can download and install the app.

5. **Tap Accept and Download in the Samsung Gear Manager window (see in Figure 2-11).**

Your smartphone takes a little time to download and install the app. After the Gear Manager app is installed, the Gear Manager entry in the list no longer shows the Download icon. Instead, you see the Open icon, as shown in Figure 2-12.

6. **Tap the icon to start the Gear Manager app.**

The Welcome screen appears, as shown in Figure 2-13, and the app asks you to continue the Gear S2 setup process by tapping Connect to Gear in the Welcome screen.

If your smartphone doesn't have Bluetooth turned on already, you'll see the Turn on Bluetooth window. The app has saved you the hassle of going into the Settings screen to turn on your Bluetooth service; all you have to do is tap OK in the window.

Your smartphone and the Gear S2 take a few seconds to pair up with each other. When both devices have paired, your smartphone screen displays the Bluetooth Pairing Request window. Complete the pairing process by tapping OK in the window.

Samsung Gear takes a few more seconds to install companion apps that the Samsung Gear app needs to function. In the meantime, the Gear S2 shows the Setting Up screen. After a few seconds, tap the Agree to Terms of the End User License

FIGURE 2-10:
The Download icon looks like a down arrow inside a circle.

FIGURE 2-11:
You have to accept the terms to download the app.

Agreement check box and then tap the Agree to All check box. Then tap Done, as shown in Figure 2-14.

Now the Manage Notifications screen appears (see Figure 2-15) so that you can tell Gear Manager how to manage notifications from smartwatch apps that are preinstalled on your Gear S2.

The Open icon looks like a right-pointing triangle (or a Play icon) inside a circle.

REMEMBER

The word *notification* in this context has a straightforward definition: It's information generated by an app that will appear on your Gear S2 screen in place of the actual clock or any other app you're viewing. If you're itching to learn more about notifications, bookmark this page and skip ahead to Chapter 5. I don't mind.

Swipe up and down to view all the apps on the Gear S2 that will give you notifications on your smartwatch. Fourteen apps are selected by default; selected apps display a green check box containing a white check mark to the left of the app icon.

You can turn off notifications for an app by tapping the check box to the left of the selected app icon; the check box turns white. If you want to turn on notifications for an app, tap the white check box to turn the check box green and add the white check mark.

If you prefer to receive notifications from all your apps, tap the All check box that appears above the list shown in Figure 2-15. Above the All check box, the Limit Notifications option is on, so you won't see the selected apps in the list of notifications on your

FIGURE 2-13:
You can't connect the Gear to your smartphone until you tell the app you're ready to connect.

Gear S2 screen. If you want to see those notifications, tap Limit Notifications to change the blue ON slider button to a gray OFF slider button.

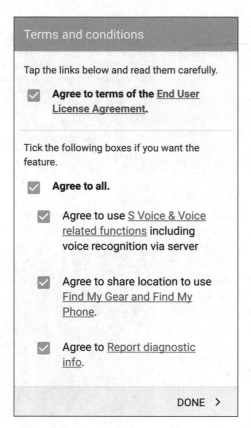

FIGURE 2-14:
Agree to everything to get access to your precious Gear S2.

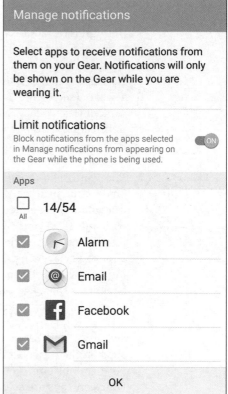

FIGURE 2-15:
The All check box appears above the Alarm app notification check box on the screen.

When you're all done, tap OK at the bottom of the screen.

Now the Gear S2 screen appears on your smartphone (see Figure 2-16) so that you can view one of the various options for changing your apps layout on the smartwatch, copy music tracks and photos to your Gear S2, change smartwatch settings, and find your Gear S2 in case you misplaced it. (You can learn more about accessing all those options in Chapter 4.)

At the bottom of the screen, a number appears to the right of the Samsung Gear Apps entry in the list. This number tells you how many new apps are available to download and use on the Gear S2, which is 8 in the example shown in Figure 2-16. The actual number of apps you can install may be different, depending on how many apps Samsung wants you to know about.

If you swipe up on the screen, you see three of the apps that you can install featured in the Gear Apps section. Tap one of the tiles to view more information about the app in the Galaxy Apps screen.

REMEMBER

You don't have to turn on your Android smartphone every time you turn on the Gear S2. If you're using your Gear S2 through your telecommunication company's 3G or 4G network, you can still receive email messages as well as send and receive voice calls. However, if you have only a Bluetooth connection on your Gear S2 and you don't turn on your smartphone when you turn on your smartwatch, you won't be able to receive email messages or voicemail notifications on your Gear S2.

Using the setup wizard on the Gear S2

After you install the Gear Manager app on your smartphone, you can turn your attention back to the Gear S2. The setup wizard appears automatically on the Gear S2 screen to show you how to use your smartwatch. Tap the screen and then follow each step in the wizard to learn how to swipe on the screen and move the bezel. If you have to put the Gear S2 down as you're going through the wizard, the screen turns off to save power. No worries: Just press the Power button to turn the screen back on.

After the wizard finishes setting up your Gear S2, you see the default Modern Utility watch face on the screen, shown in Figure 2-17, telling you what time it is. If you don't like the watch face, don't worry. You can choose from plenty of other faces, as you find out in Chapter 3.

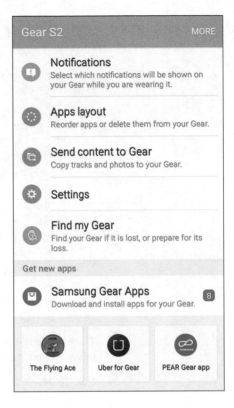

FIGURE 2-16:
Three featured apps appear at the bottom of the Gear Manager screen.

FIGURE 2-17:
The watch tells you the time, just like . . . a watch.

Sporting Your Slick Smartwatch

The Gear S2 is designed to look like a real watch, so don't say you're surprised that you have to put the Gear S2 on just as you do a regular watch.

Maybe you've never put on a watch before. Don't laugh. If you've grown up with smartphones, you may not have needed a watch and have always just checked your phone for the time. So if you're one of these watch-less souls, don't be embarrassed. I've got your back . . . and your wrist.

Figure 2-18 shows you the different parts of the Gear S2. The case is flanked by two straps, each with a different height.

Here's how to attach the Gear S2 to your wrist:

1. **Place the bottom of the case on the top of your wrist.**

2. **Place the large wrist strap inside the small strap's buckle.**

3. **Pull the large strap until the watch is snug (but not tight) around your wrist.**

4. **Insert the large strap under the free loops on the short band to keep the strap from flopping around.**

Easy peasy.

But, you say, what if the large strap is a little too long for your wrist? Samsung thought about you and included a shorter large strap. The company also made it easy for you to replace the standard large strap with this shorter version. For this example, I've replace the standard large strap on my Gear S2 Classic with the smaller one that came in the box.

If you're viewing the Gear S2 screen, flip over the smartwatch so that you see the back of the case and the back of the wrist straps. At

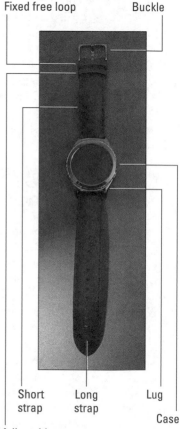

Fixed free loop   Buckle

Short strap   Long strap   Lug

Case

Adjustable free loop

FIGURE 2-18:
The technical terms for all the parts of the Gear S2.

the end of the band that connects to the case, look for a spring-loaded bar (spring bar for short) that's covered mostly by the band itself so that it doesn't slip off. The ends of the bar fit into the lug holes. *Lug* is the term for the two brackets at the top and bottom of the case that holds the bands.

You can release the spring bar from the lug hole using the spring bar release button, shown in Figure 2-19.

Remove the strap by pulling the spring bar release button to the left and holding the button there as you pull away from the case. One end of the spring bar appears on the right side of the band, as shown in Figure 2-20.

With one end of the spring bar free, pull the watch band to the right to free the other side of the spring bar from its lug hole and away from the watch case.

Now it's time to get your new wrist strap and be sure that the back of the strap (that is, the side that will rest on your wrist) faces up.

Insert one end of the spring bar into the left lug hole. Now pull the spring bar button to the left so that the end of the spring bar on the right side of the band disappears, as shown in Figure 2-21.

Move the band toward the watch case until the spring bar is parallel to the bottom of the watch case. Now release your finger from the release button. The spring bar is connected to the lug (see Figure 2-22).

FIGURE 2-19:
The spring bar release button is on the right side of the spring bar after you flip the watch over.

FIGURE 2-20:
There's one end of the spring bar.

FIGURE 2-21:
You can't see the end of the spring bar that you just inserted because the bar is hidden by the band.

Give the strap a tug to make sure that the strap is secure. If it isn't, one of two things happens: The spring bar attaches to the lug hole with a little click, or the right side of the strap (or the entire strap) detaches, and you have to try attaching the strap again.

When your new wrist strap is secure, put the Gear S2 on and see how it feels with the shorter large strap. You can switch back to the regular-sized large strap whenever you want or even buy another strap from Samsung or a third party. Just type **Samsung Gear S2 straps** in your favorite web search engine and have fun shopping.

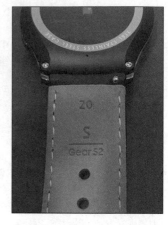

FIGURE 2-22:
Both ends of the spring bar are now connected to the lug.

Turning Off Your Gear S2

When you're satisfied with how the Gear S2 feels on your wrist and you decide that you want to take off your smartwatch and let it recharge, you need to turn off the Gear S2 itself.

All you have to do is press and hold on the Power button on the right side of the smartwatch case. After a couple of seconds, tap Power Off on the screen (see Figure 2-23).

The Samsung logo appears for a couple of seconds and then the screen turns off using a slick animation that makes it seem like you own a secret agent watch from 1960s TV shows. Now you can put the Gear S2 on the charger, charge up the battery, and get ready for Chapter 3, where you find out how to make your Gear S2 truly your own.

FIGURE 2-23:
The Power Off option appears in the center of the screen.

Chapter 3

Customizing Your Gear S2

A re you as excited as a 6-month-old sitting up by herself for the first time? After all, it's time to actually play with the Gear S2 and learn how you can change its settings so that it works the way you want.

The screen that you're likely to see the most on your Gear S2 is the clock, so this chapter starts by showing you how to change the various features of the clock. You can customize the clock face and hands, as well as other features such as the one that tracks your steps. This chapter also shows you how to access and change other Gear settings. Finally, you learn about options within each setting so that you know how get the Gear S2 to do your bidding.

Transforming Your (Watch) Face

When you look at the screen of your Gear S2 as it displays the clock, you're looking at a representation of an analog clock. I suspect you remember what you learned about clocks when you were a kid, so I won't bore you with a recap.

The Gear S2 can display a number of different analog clock design styles, or faces. The default clock face that you see on your Gear S2 depends on the model you have. For example, my black Gear S2 Classic uses the Modern Utility clock face.

If you prefer a digital clock that displays numbers instead of hands and a dial, you can choose from a number of digital clock faces as well. What's more, if you don't like any of the faces that come preinstalled on your Gear S2, you can shop for more faces from the Samsung Galaxy Apps store on your Android smartphone. Some of the faces in the Galaxy Apps store require you to purchase them before you can download them and then install them from your smartphone to your Gear S2.

Viewing available watch faces

You can easily access the Settings list and view the watch faces right on your Gear S2. Follow these steps:

1. **Swipe the screen from right to left (or rotate the bezel to the right) until you see the Quick Access screen, shown in Figure 3-1.**

2. **Tap Settings.**

    The Display menu is highlighted in the center of the Settings screen (see Figure 3-2).

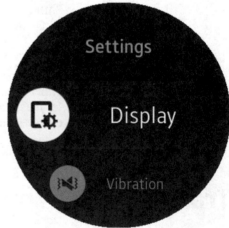

FIGURE 3-1:
The Settings icon appears at the bottom of the screen.

FIGURE 3-2:
The Display text and icon are large and white to indicate that you can open this menu by tapping Display.

3. **Tap Display.**

   Within the Display menu that appears, you see the Watch Faces option highlighted in white in the center of the screen (see Figure 3-3).

4. **Tap Watch Faces to open the gallery of faces.**

   On my black Gear S2 Classic, a sample of the Modern Utility watch face appears in the middle of the screen, as shown in Figure 3-4. The faces row, which is a row of 15 small circles, appears at the top of the screen. The faces row represents the number of watch faces you can choose from.

FIGURE 3-3:
The Watch Faces menu option is in the center of the screen.

FIGURE 3-4:
The Modern Utility face name scrolls so that you can see the entire name.

   The Modern Utility face is the second face from the left in the faces row. As you move to a different face, the associated circle turns white to show you where you are in relation to the other watch faces.

5. **Swipe left and right on the screen or rotate the bezel to the left and right to view all the faces you can choose.**

   Table 3-1 lists all the faces available on the Gear S2.

TABLE 3-1

Watch Faces

Icon	Watch Face	Description
	Classic	Shows not only the current time and date but also the current month and current day of the week. When you're viewing the Modern Utility face, you can view this face by moving the bezel to the left or swiping from left to right on the screen.
	Modern Utility	Shows the current time and date, your battery strength status, and how many steps you've taken while the watch has been on.
	Neon	A very simple and cool face: All you get are the minute, hour, and second hands, as well as the current date.
	Chronograph	Displays the current date, an analog clock with a minute and hour hand, a smaller second clock, and two small stopwatches.
	World Time	Shows your current time as well as the time for two different cities. The default cities shown are London and Beijing. I tell you how to change the cities in Chapter 5.
	Activity Bubbles	Contains two bubbles: one for sitting and one for standing. Depending on your activity, one of the two bubbles gets larger. For example, if you're walking around, the green bubble is larger.
	Heart Wave	Shows you your current pulse as well as the highest and lowest pulse rates recorded while you've had the watch on.
	Pixel Heart	Shows you the digital time as well as your current heart rate.
	Digital	Shows the time, the current date, and how many steps you've taken since the watch has been turned on.
	Activity Sparkles	Shows the digital time text in front of a lot of multicolored dots, or sparkles. When you move around while wearing the watch, the sparkles move around. The sparkles move more quickly as your activity becomes more vigorous.

Icon	Watch Face	Description
	Large	Shows the digital time in large text.
	Nike Watchface	Shows an analog clock as well as information relevant to your latest run, such as how many miles you've covered.
	CNNDigital	Shows the current digital time, the current date, and a slide show of the day's brief news headlines.
	Bloomberg	Shows an analog clock as well as the current stock market indexes' rise or fall in percentage terms.

The last watch face screen, which is the rightmost circle in the faces row, allows you to add a face. Stay tuned, because I tell you how to add a face in the "Getting yourself a new face" section, later in this chapter.

Applying a watch face

When you see a watch face you like, just tap the watch face on the screen. After a second or two, you see your watch face on the screen, telling you the current time.

REMEMBER

If you don't take any action in the Watch Faces screen after 15 seconds, the watch turns off and doesn't apply any new watch face. You need to press the Power button and repeat the steps to open the Watch Faces screen. So if you need some more time to make a decision, go ahead and move between faces every 10 seconds or so.

Stylizing Your Face

Samsung has anticipated the need for you to scratch the itch that is the ability to change different features of your watch face. But you don't just change it; you *stylize* it. (Ooooo.)

Not all faces can be stylized, and the features you can stylize depend on the face you've selected. For the example in this section, I stylize the Modern Utility face that comes as the default on my black Gear S2 Classic smartwatch. (If you want, you can stylize by using the Gear Manager app instead, as I cover Chapter 4.)

Start by opening the Watch Faces screen. (If you need a refresher, see "Viewing available watch faces," earlier in this chapter.) If your watch face can be stylized, the word *Stylize* appears under the face, as shown in Figure 3-5.

Tap Stylize to open the Stylize screen, shown in Figure 3-6. Now swipe right and left on the screen to view the five features available with this face:

FIGURE 3-5:
The Stylize option appears at the bottom of the screen.

- » **Dial:** Shows the watch face background color as well as the minute tick marks that appear on the outer edge of the screen. You may also see numbers with these tick marks.

- » **Hands:** Displays the minute and second hands, as you may have guessed.

- » **Battery:** Displays the current battery level from 1 (riding the ragged edge of emptiness) to 100 (full).

- » **Steps:** Shows the number of steps you've taken since you put the watch on.

FIGURE 3-6:
The sample face shows you how your new dial will look.

- » **Date:** Displays the current date of the month.

When you see the feature you want to change, rotate the bezel to the right to view all the different options. As you rotate the bezel, the new option appears onscreen. For example, if you're changing the dial, you see each dial onscreen as you rotate the bezel (see Figure 3-6).

The blue area within the curved scroll bar on the right side of the screen also moves up and down as you rotate the bezel. When you find a style you like, tap OK near the bottom of the screen. If you decide that you're okay with default dial style after all, press the Home button on the side of the Gear S2.

Getting yourself a new face

If you get bored with your current watch face and the other preinstalled faces don't excite you, no worries: You can use the Gear S2 to find a new face in the Samsung Galaxy Apps store. However, the Galaxy Apps store is available only on your Android smartphone, so you need to have your smartphone at the ready before you shop for a new face.

You can add a face straight from your Gear S2 by following these handy-dandy instructions:

1. **Press the Home button.**

    The Apps screen appears.

2. **Tap the Settings icon in the Apps screen that appears.**

3. **Tap Display in the Settings screen that appears.**

4. **Tap Watch Faces in the Display screen that appears.**

Now you can swipe from right to left on the Watch Faces screen or rotate the bezel to the right until you see the plus icon on the screen (see Figure 3-7). Now tap the plus icon.

You can view all the additional watch faces in the Face Templates screen by swiping right to left on the screen or by rotating the bezel to the right. Though all the faces are available for you to select in the Watch Faces screen, you can also select the watch face you want in the Face Templates screen by tapping the face on the screen.

FIGURE 3-7:
In Watch Faces, rotate the bezel until the plus icon appears in the center in the screen.

If you don't like any of the faces, swipe from right to left or rotate the bezel to the right until you see the Get More Watch Faces screen, shown in Figure 3-8. Now tap the screen.

The Gear S2 tells you to get watch faces on your smartphone and sends a message to your smartphone to open the Watch Faces page within the Samsung Galaxy Apps app. The Watch Faces page, shown in Figure 3-9, displays a list of all the watch faces you can download.

Each entry in the list shown in Figure 3-9 includes the name of the watch face, an image of the watch face, the name of the developer, the cost of the face (if any), and reviews from other Galaxy Apps users. The reviews are rated with gold stars ranging from 1 star (you may want to look elsewhere) to 5 (run, don't walk, to get this face). If the watch face is already installed on your Gear S2, you see the word *Installed* instead of the price.

Tap an entry in the list to view more information about the face, including developer information, related apps or faces from the developer, and individual user reviews.

If you decide you don't want a watch face, tap the Back icon in the upper-left corner of the screen. You return to the Watch Faces screen within the Gear Manager app.

Scrubbing a face

If you see watch faces that you find as welcome on your Gear S2 as a spider is in your home, you'll be pleased to know that you can delete one or more faces on your smartwatch. You cannot

FIGURE 3-8:
The screen invites you to tap it so that you can shop for more watch faces.

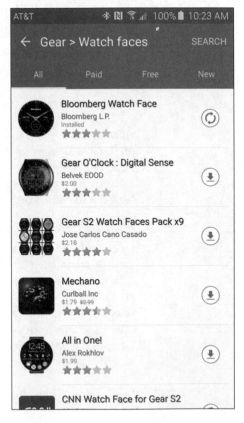

FIGURE 3-9:
Swipe the smartphone screen up and down to view the list of all watch faces from which to choose.

delete your currently selected face (after all, you need one for the Gear S2 to work), but you can delete any other face by following these steps:

1. **Go to Settings and tap Display⇨Watch Faces to open the Watch Faces screen.**

2. **Swipe back and forth on the screen (or rotate the bezel) until you find the face that you want to delete.**

3. **In the upper-right corner of the watch face image, tap the Delete icon, shown in Figure 3-10.**

   When you tap the Delete icon, the face disappears immediately.

FIGURE 3-10:
The Delete icon is a white circle with a red minus sign inside it.

TIP

If you regret deleting a watch face, cheer up. You can add the face again on either the Gear S2 or in the Gear Manager app on your smartphone. (See Chapter 4 to find out how.)

Making Your Gear Your Own

In addition to letting you change the watch face, the Gear S2 offers plenty of settings that you can change. It's nice to know what those settings are before you change them, though. You can access Settings by swiping right to left on the screen or rotating the bezel to the right until you see the Quick Access screen, shown in Figure 3-11. Now tap Settings.

Swipe up and down on the screen or rotate the bezel to the left and right to view all the settings within the Settings list. As you move up and down the list, the selected setting text is both white and larger as well as centered on the screen. Tap a setting to view a list of options associated with it.

FIGURE 3-11:
The Settings icon appears at the bottom of the screen.

The following sections explain each setting, and I throw in a discussion of available options within each setting.

Setting the Display options

Within the Display options screen, shown in Figure 3-12, the Watch Faces option is selected by default.

Swipe up and down in the options screen to view and change one of three settings options within the options screen.

FIGURE 3-12:
The Watch Faces option displays in the center of the screen.

Watch Always On

Tap Watch Always On to keep the Gear S2 on all the time. With this option on, the Gear S2 won't turn off after 15 seconds of inactivity. Instead, you see the current time (either the analog hands or the digital time) onscreen.

After you tap the Watch Always On option, a warning appears on screen saying that keeping the watch always on significantly increases battery consumption. Tap the check mark icon on the right side of the screen to keep the watch always on, or tap the Cancel icon (it looks like an *X*) on the left side of the screen to put the Gear S2 in sleep mode when you're not using the smartwatch.

When you set the watch to Always On, a green On icon appears to the right of the Watch Always On text. When the watch isn't set to Always On, a gray Off icon appears to the right of that text.

Notification Indicator

This option is on by default and will turn the Gear S2 screen on and vibrate when it receives a notification. When you lift your arm, you see the notification on the screen. After a few seconds, the notification message closes and the watch face tells you the current time.

Brightness

This option sets the brightness of your screen. The default value is 7. Rotate the bezel to the left and right to change the brightness level. When you're finished, press the Back button on the right side of the watch to return to the Display options screen.

Screen Timeout

The screen turns off after 15 seconds by default. After you tap Screen Timeout, you can change the time to 30 seconds, 1 minute, or 5 minutes. After you select a time, you return to the Display options screen, and the time underneath the Screen Timeout option shows the time interval you selected.

Font

You can change the font style to Choco Cooky, Cool Jazz, or Rosemary (yes, I'm serious), or you can just keep the Default font. You can also change the font size to Small, the default Medium, or Large. When you change the font style, size, or both, you see your font changes in the Font screen so that you can decide whether you like the changes.

Setting the Vibration options

Tap the Vibration setting to open the Vibration options menu (see Figure 3-13), which lets you change both the vibration intensity and the length of the buzz when the Gear S2 has something interesting to share with you.

You have two options from which to choose onscreen.

Intensity

You can choose how intense the vibration is. The default is Strong, but you can also tap Weak for a softer vibration, or None for no vibration. After you tap Strong or Weak, you feel the watch vibrate so that you know how intense the Strong and Weak vibrations are.

FIGURE 3-13:
The Strong text appears underneath the Intensity option so that you know the current vibration intensity is strong.

Long Buzz

Tap Long Buzz if you need the vibration to be a little longer to get you to take a look at your watch to see what's happening.

Setting Device options

In the Device menu, you can choose from the Double Press Home Key and Wake-Up Gesture options, as shown in Figure 3-14.

Double Press Home Key

If you want to open your favorite app on the Gear S2 quickly instead of having to swipe the screen or rotate the bezel, you can select an app that you can open when you press the Home button twice. When you tap Double Press Home Key in the Device screen, you see a list of options that includes the default None option. You can select from one of the following apps:

FIGURE 3-14:
The Double Press Home Key option is highlighted by default.

>> **Last App:** Opens the screen within the last app you had open before you returned to the watch screen. For example, if you have the Device options screen open and you press the Home button to return to the watch screen, press the Home button twice within the Home screen and you'll go back to the Device options screen. (Slick, no?)

>> **Recent Apps:** Opens the Recent Apps screen. I tell you how to use Recent Apps in Chapter 10.

>> **Alarm:** Alarm is what you expect: You can add an alarm so that your watch will make noise when the alarm is triggered. If you want to postpone the alarm for five minutes, you can activate the Snooze option. You can also delete an alarm when you have no further use for it.

>> **Bloomberg:** Bloomberg shows you a summary of your stock portfolio and gives you a recap of the latest news from the business world.

>> **Buddy:** Buddy is an app that allows you to select your favorite contacts from your Contacts list. Within the Buddy app, you can tap your buddy to quickly call or send a message to that person.

>> **CNN:** CNN is a popular online news source (not so much on TV) that delivers up-to-the-minute news updates to your Gear S2.

>> **Email:** Email is a straightforward app that synchronizes with the email accounts on your smartphone and then displays a brief summary your email message on the screen. Tap the summary on the screen to read the entire message and reply to it by either speaking or typing your reply on the Gear S2.

>> **ESPN:** ESPN shows you a summary of the latest sports scores and news. You need to install the ESPN Companion for Gear app on your smartphone to use the ESPN app on your Gear S2.

>> **Find My Phone:** Find My Phone is a useful little app. You open the app, tap Start, and then listen for your smartphone to make noise. The smartphone screen turns on, too.

>> **Gallery:** Gallery allows you to view images you've captured on your Gear S2. You can capture an image by holding down the Home button and then swiping left or right on the screen.

>> **Maps:** Maps shows you your current location on a very small map. You can also search for a specific location and for businesses or features near you, such as the nearest lake where you can enjoy a day out.

>> **Messages:** The Messages app allows you to view messages and then either type a reply or call the messenger back.

>> **Music Player:** Music Player is Samsung's default app for playing music stored on your Gear S2 as well as on your smartphone.

>> **News Briefing:** News Briefing is a news aggregator from Flipboard and provides you with a summary of the latest news. Swipe up and down to view leading news stories in a variety of categories.

>> **Phone:** The Phone app shows you notifications for incoming calls so that you can grab your smartphone and take the call (or not). The app also synchronizes the Contacts list on your smartphone, enabling you to initiate a call from the Contacts list or just tap the phone number on your watch. If you have the Standard Gear S2 or the black Gear S2 Classic that is supported by a data carrier, you can also respond and talk on your watch. Otherwise, you need to get out your smartphone to receive your call.

>> **Nike+ Running:** The Nike+ Running app uses sensors on the back of the Gear S2 to monitor your vital signs as you run and keep track of your statistics to help you improve your running performance.

>> **S Health:** S Health tracks your physical activity and measures your pulse while you move by using the sensors on the back of the Gear S2. You find out how to set up and use S Health in Chapter 9.

- **S Voice:** S Voice is the default voice command app that lets you tell your Gear S2 what to do. You see how to make the Gear S2 obey your every command in Chapter 8.

- **Samsung Milk Music:** Samsung Milk Music is Samsung's streaming music service that allows you to play music on not only your Gear S2 but also your smartphone.

- **Schedule:** The Schedule app shows you your upcoming appointment as well as a brief note about your following appointment, if you have one.

- **Settings:** The Settings app allows you to view and change Gear S2 settings, which you're learning all about in this chapter.

- **Stopwatch:** Stopwatch lets you time an event. You can start the stopwatch, pause it, restart it, and stop it. You can also view a stopwatch log to compare times from previous events.

- **Timer:** Timer allows you to set the amount of time for the countdown, and when the timer reaches zero the watch makes noise to let you know your time is up.

- **Voice Memo:** Voice Memo lets you record a voice memo on your Gear S2 that you can play back later. You can also save the voice memo as a text file to read.

- **Weather:** The Weather app shows you the current weather information for your location. You can also add another location and view the current conditions in that location.

- **World Clock:** World Clock allows you to add one or more cities around the world and show the current time in the city or cities.

Wake-Up Gesture

The Gear S2 turns off the screen after a few seconds of inactivity, which is smart because turning off the screen saves battery juice. By default, the Gear S2 turns the screen on and shows you the current time on your selected watch face when you raise your arm and look at the watch.

If you don't want the Gear S2 to wake up unless you press the Power button, tap Wake-up Gesture. In the Wake-up Gesture options screen, tap Wake-up Gesture to turn off the wake up gesture. Then you can return to the Device screen by pressing the Back button.

Answering a call

When your Gear S2 detects that you're receiving a phone call, you see a screen with Answer and Reject icons. You can answer a call by swiping the green Answer icon from left to right to answer the call and then talk either on your smartphone or on your Gear S2 if your smartwatch is either a Standard or black Gear S2 Classic model and you bought said model from a phone carrier.

One of the (never-ending list of) cool things about your Gear S2 is that you can also use your voice to tell your smartwatch to answer or reject a call. Within the Call menu, only the Voice Answer option is available to set.

FIGURE 3-15:
The message that tells you how to answer or reject a call using your voice.

When you tap that option, a message appears on the screen (see Figure 3-15) that tells you how to answer or reject a call: by saying Answer or Reject, respectively.

If answering or rejecting calls with your voice works for you, tap the check mark icon on the right side of the screen. If not, tap the Cancel icon (it has an *X* in it) on the left side of the screen.

Making network connections

The Connections options screen, shown in Figure 3-16, allows you to change options for the Bluetooth, Wi-Fi, and Near Field Communication (NFC) settings so that you can turn these options on and off as well as control related features.

Bluetooth

To open the Bluetooth options screen, tap Bluetooth in the options list. The Gear S2 turns on Bluetooth by default after you set up your smartwatch for

FIGURE 3-16:
The word On appears underneath the Bluetooth setting to let you know the Bluetooth service is on.

the first time. You can turn off Bluetooth by tapping Bluetooth on the screen. If you have a Bluetooth headset, you can connect your headset to your Gear S2 and listen to music stored on your smartwatch. Just tap BT Headset to have the Gear S2 search for your headset. When your Gear S2 finds the headset, your smartwatch connects with the headset automatically so that you can start grooving.

Wi-Fi

Tap Wi-Fi in the options list to open the Wi-Fi options screen. The Gear S2 turns Wi-Fi on automatically after you set it up for the first time. Tap Wi-Fi on that same screen to turn off Wi-Fi.

By default, the Gear S2 connects to your smartphone using the Bluetooth service, so the Gear S2 uses your smartphone's Wi-Fi connection as well. However, if you turn off your smartphone, your widgets won't be able to connect to the Internet and give you correct information, such as the correct temperature in the Weather widget.

Samsung has your back (or is it your wrist?). Search for available Wi-Fi networks by swiping up in the Wi-Fi options screen and then tapping Wi-Fi Networks in the menu. The Gear S2 scans for available Wi-Fi networks and displays a list in the Wi-Fi Networks screen. You can view all entries in the list by swiping up and down on the screen or rotating the bezel left and right. If you can't find a network, tap Scan at the bottom of the screen.

When you find a Wi-Fi network, connect to it by tapping the network name. You may need to type the password (which is a challenge on the Gear S2, as I explain in Chapter 3). After you type the password or enter any network-specific information on the screen, tap Connect.

After a second or two, the connection screen appears for another second or two. The Wi-Fi network in the Wi-Fi Networks screen shows that you're connected. Press the Back button three times (just as with the ruby slippers) to return to the Connections options screen.

If you find that you don't have a Wi-Fi network, press the Back button three times until you reach the Connections options screen. Then you can turn the Bluetooth service back on and connect to your smartphone's Wi-Fi network.

TIP

If you turn on the Bluetooth service while you're connected to a Wi-Fi network, the Gear S2 automatically disconnects from the Wi-Fi network and then turns on the Bluetooth service.

REMEMBER

If you connect to an open Wi-Fi network, you open the possibility for evildoers to intercept the data being transferred over the network. It's always good practice to connect to a secure Wi-Fi network whenever possible, no matter whether you're connecting to a Wi-Fi network with your Gear S2 or with your Android smartphone.

NFC

NFC (no, not the pro football conference; it stands for Near Field Communication) is a cool new feature that allows you to pay for goods and services right on your watch using a supported pay feature such as Samsung Pay, which Samsung plans to make available in the United States sometime in 2016.

NFC is turned on by default, but you can turn it off by tapping NFC in the options list and then tapping NFC in the NFC options screen. You can also pay for an item from within the NFC options screen by tapping Tap and Pay. If you don't have a payment app installed on your watch, you see a screen informing you of that fact.

TIP

Samsung Pay on the Gear S2 was already available in some countries before its availability in the United States, so check the Samsung website (www.samsung.com) to see whether you can use Samsung Pay with your Gear S2 where you live.

Locking your screen

If you live with others, or if you're in a public place or even a hotel room, you may not want people to gain access to your Gear S2 when you don't have it on your wrist. To ensure your privacy, you can add a personal information number (PIN), which means that anyone — including you — will have to enter that PIN to unlock your Gear S2 screen.

To set up a screen lock, follow these steps:

1. **In the Connections options screen, tap Screen Lock in the setting options list.**

   The Screen Lock screen appears.

2. **Tap PIN.**

   You see the screen shown in Figure 3-17.

3. **Type a four-digit PIN using the number keys that appear around the periphery of the screen.**

4. **Type your PIN again to confirm that it's correct.**

The next time you look at your Gear S2, or after you turn the watch off and on again, you'll still be able to see the current time on the watch screen. The lock icon appears at the top of the watch screen (that is, at the 12 o'clock position) so that you know the screen is locked.

When you try to access any functions, such as when you press the Home button to access the Apps screen, you see the Enter PIN screen, which lets you type your PIN and unlock your screen. After you type your correct PIN, the watch screen appears again, but now you can access all functions of your Gear S2. However, if the screen turns off, you need to type in your PIN again to access the functions of your smartwatch.

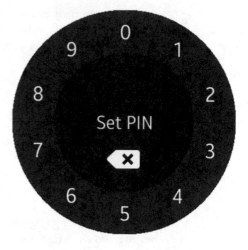

FIGURE 3-17:
Create your PIN by using the keypad around the periphery of the screen.

TIP

If you misplace your Gear S2 and the screen is locked with a PIN, you know that someone else will have a very hard time getting access. However, you also likely want to find the watch to get it back (and figure out who has it), so you need to use the Find My Gear option in the Gear Manager app on your smartphone so that you have a good chance of finding your wayward smartwatch. You learn more about the Gear Manager app in Chapter 4.

Choosing your input preferences

The Gear S2 uses the preinstalled Samsung keyboard by default. You can, however, download third-party keyboards from the Galaxy Apps store on your smartphone. You'll likely find the Samsung keyboard to be plenty good enough, plus it comes with a number of options that you can change. To see those options, tap Input in the Connections options screen.

In the Input options screen that appears, tap Keyboard Settings. Within the Keyboard Settings screen, tap Samsung Keyboard. Now you can view all six Samsung Keyboard options in the Samsung Keyboard options screen, shown in Figure 3-18. The next sections describe those options.

English (US)

When you type information, you see the default row/column keyboard layout that's similar to what you find on a smartphone dial pad. Tap English (US) to change between the default row/column layout and a rotary keyboard layout where the letter and number keys are located around the periphery of the screen.

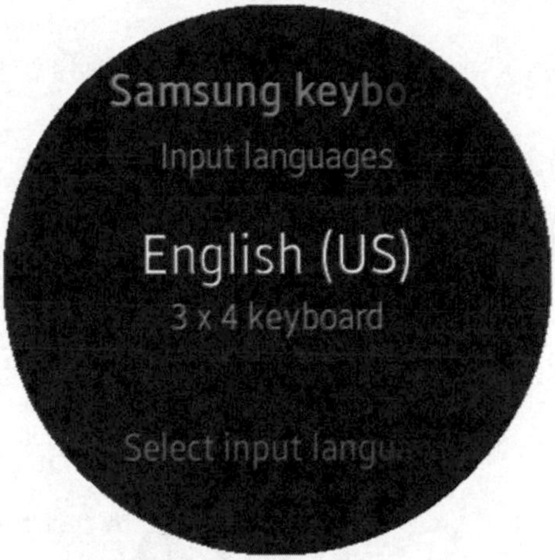

Select Input Languages

You can select one or more languages from the list so that you can type special characters that are unique to a language, such as the c-cedilla letter in French. Some common languages, such as French and Spanish, are installed on the Gear S2 by default, but if your desired language isn't included on your watch, tap that language's name and Samsung will automatically install it on your smartwatch.

FIGURE 3-18:
Swipe up and down to view all options in the Samsung Keyboard options screen.

REMEMBER

If you've filled your Gear S2 with a lot of apps and other data that take up much of your memory, you may not be able to download a new language. In that case, you need to decide what to remove from your Gear S2 to provide enough room for your new language.

Check Update

This option enables you to access the Samsung website and retrieve language files that Samsung has developed recently so that you can use one of these new languages on the Gear S2.

Smart Typing

The Smart Typing options screen allows you to change the following options:

>> **Turn predictive text on and off.** Predictive text is on by default and recommends words that the Gear S2 thinks you're trying to type so that you can save some time. Be aware that predictive text can lead to the dreaded autocorrect failures whereby you send someone unintentionally confusing or hilarious text (and perhaps have it become an Internet meme).

>> **Turn personalized data on and off.** Personalized data, which is on by default, is data you enter that the Gear S2 remembers, such as the spelling of your name.

>> **Change the auto-replace text language.** You use this option to correct spelling for words in your preferred language.

>> **Turn auto-capitalize, auto spacing, and auto punctuation on or off.** All these features, which are on by default, enable your Gear S2 to automatically fix any problems with capitalization, spacing between words, and punctuation.

Key-Tap Feedback

If you want to feel the Gear S2 vibrate every time you tap a keyboard key, tap Vibration in the Key-Tap Feedback screen.

Reset Settings

Tap this option to reset all keyboard settings except for downloaded languages. In the Reset Settings screen, you reset the settings by tapping the blue Confirm icon (it has a check mark in it) on the right side of the screen. If you change your mind, tap the Cancel icon (it has an X in it) on the left side of the screen.

Setting Power Saving mode

In case you can't charge your Gear S2 right away, Samsung has given you the Power Saving setting so that you can squeeze the most juice out of your battery. To turn this setting on, go to the Connections options screen and tap Power Saving. The Power Saving screen, as shown in Figure 3-19, appears and tells you what this mode does to save power.

Those power saving strategies include:

>> Using a grayscale Home screen instead of full color and a digital clock on the Home screen instead of an analog one

FIGURE 3-19:
Swipe up and down the screen to read what the Gear S2 does to keep your smartwatch running.

- » Limiting functions to receiving calls, messages, and notifications

- » Turning off Wi-Fi

- » Limiting the smartwatch's overall performance

If you decide against saving power, tap the Cancel icon (it has an *X* in it) on the left side of the screen. Turn on Power Saving mode by tapping the Confirm icon (it has a check mark in it) on the right side of the screen.

The power saving Home screen comes on and shows you the current time at the top of the bland, monochrome screen. In the center of the screen are the following three icons (from left to right):

- » **Call icon:** Tap to review received calls

- » **Battery icon:** Shows the current battery strength percentage

- » **Messages icon:** Tap to review received messages and notifications

Turn off Power Saving mode by tapping Off at the bottom of the screen and then tapping the Confirm icon at the right side of the confirmation screen that appears. Your regular Home screen returns and displays the current time.

Getting and sending info about your Gear

Tap Gear Info in the Connections options screen to select from one of the following options in the Gear Info options screen, shown in Figure 3-20:

- » **About Device:** View information about the device, including the model number, serial number, software version, and Bluetooth and Wi-Fi addresses.

- » **Report Diagnostics:** Have the Gear S2 report its activity to Samsung on a regular basis. This option is turned on by default, but tap Report Diagnostics to turn this feature off.

FIGURE 3-20:
Swipe up and down in the Gear Info screen to view all the options.

>> **Reset Gear:** You can reset your Gear S2 in one of two ways. You can perform a light reset that preserves media files and personal data but deletes down-loaded apps and reinstalls all default apps. You can also perform a factory reset that deletes all files on the Gear S2 and reinstalls the files so that your smartwatch looks and feels as it did when you first took it out of the box.

>> **Debugging:** The Gear S2 debugger reads log data, copies files to and from your computer, and installs apps without notifying you first. Tap Debugging to turn this feature on. If you want to use a computer with your Gear S2 for debugging purposes, the Tizen Experts website has an excellent article about how to connect your computer with your Gear S2 at `http://www.tizenexperts.com/2015/12/how-to-deploy-to-gear-s2-smartwatch/`.

Return to the Connections options screen by pressing the Back button. If you want to view more settings in the main Settings screen, press the Back button again. You can return to the Home screen and view the current time by pressing the Home button.

Chapter 4

Gotta Get Gear S2 into My Life

The Gear S2 is a wonderful little gadget, but the screen is small by design and we don't have one of those holographic watches (yet) that projects a large screen above your wrist. But, wait! Samsung engineers knew that they already have a larger screen in a smartphone, and Samsung marketers knew that people keep their smartphones with them at all times.

So Samsung decided to integrate the Gear Manager app with all its smartphones as well as other Android smartphones. As noted in Chapter 2, you need to download the Gear Manager app on your smartphone before you can set up your Gear S2.

In this chapter, I start by showing you how to open the Gear Manager app on your smartphone. Next, you learn how to update existing apps as well as install new apps on your Gear S2. Then it's time for the grand tour of the Gear Manager app, where you find out how to change and stylize watch faces, send content to the Gear S2, and review your settings. Finally, you see how to use the Find My Gear feature to locate your wayward Gear S2.

TIP

Not sure whether your Android smartphone plays well with your Gear S2? Call Samsung at 1-800-SAMSUNG (that's 1-800-726-7864) to talk to a real person and ask Samsung whether it supports your smartphone. If not, don't be surprised if the customer service representative happily suggests that you replace your smartphone with the latest model from Samsung.

Discovering the Gear Manager App

After you install the Gear Manager app on your smartphone, the app icon appears on a page within the Apps screen. The exact page depends on the icon layout in your Apps screen. If you've already turned on your watch, the Gear Manager app on your smartphone turns on automatically. Even if your Gear S2 is off, you can turn on the Gear Manager app anytime to learn a bit more about it, even though you won't be able to use the app to control the Gear S2 because it's, you know, off.

For this chapter, I use the Gear Manager app on my Samsung Galaxy S6 running Android 5.0.2, better known by its moniker Lollipop. (You may have a different phone or OS.) To open the Gear Manager app, start by tapping the Apps icon in the lower-right corner of the Home screen, as shown in Figure 4-1.

In the Apps screen, swipe right to left until you locate the Samsung Gear icon in the Apps screen. Next, tap the Samsung Gear icon, as shown in Figure 4-2. The icon gets your attention: It's a bright orange box that has the word Gear in it.

The Gear Manager screen contains a list of options you can choose from, including tiles of featured apps. If your Gear S2 isn't on, you see a Connect link just below the orange menu bar, as shown in Figure 4-3.

FIGURE 4-1:
The Apps icon on the Home screen.

FIGURE 4-2:
The orange Samsung Gear icon contains the word *Gear,* so you can identify it easily.

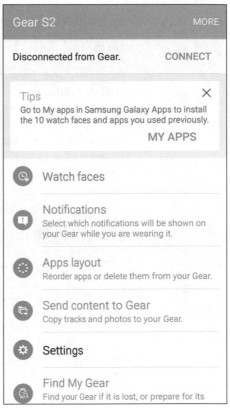

FIGURE 4-3:
The orange menu bar appears at the top of the screen.

You can connect with the Gear S2 by turning on your Gear S2 and then tapping Connect to have the app search for the smartwatch. After a few seconds, the smart-watch connects with the Gear S2 and a notification appears on your smartphone.

You can also connect to the Gear S2 by tapping the word More at the right side of the orange menu bar and then tapping Connect in the pop-up menu that appears, as shown in Figure 4-4. If you want to connect Gear Manager to another Samsung Gear device, tap Connect New Gear in the pop-up menu so that Gear Manager can scan for that device.

Getting the settings the way you want them

Before you start working with other features of the Gear Manager app, you should check its settings to make sure that the settings in both Gear Manager and on your Gear S2 are as they should be.

Tap Settings in the Gear Manager menu (refer to Figure 4-3). It's the fifth entry in the menu. In the Settings screen that appears, you see the following options (see Figure 4-5).

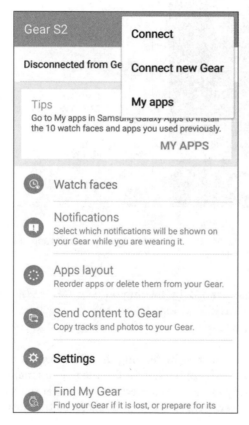

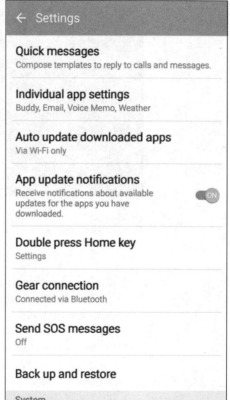

FIGURE 4-4:
The pop-up menu allows you to connect to the Gear S2 or another Samsung Gear device.

FIGURE 4-5:
The first eight Setting options appear in the Settings screen.

Quick Messages

You can select a text message to send to a caller, as well as select from one of the standard messages when you want to reject a caller for some reason, such as you can't talk because you're driving (and therefore keeping your eyes on the road as you're supposed to). If you don't like any of the preinstalled text messages, you can type separate 160-character messages call-reject messages.

Individual App Settings

You can change individual app settings for four apps that Samsung thinks you'll use most often: Buddy, Email, Voice Memo, and the Weather app. After you select the app you want to change in the Individual App Settings window, you can change the selected app's settings in the appropriate settings screen. For example, you can add another email account in the Email app. Here are more examples of what you can change:

- » **Buddy:** You can add as many as 11 of your contacts so that you can call or send messages to those favorite people with your Gear S2. You can also remove one or more contacts in the list as well as reorder the list so that your most favorite people appear at the top of the list.

- » **Email:** You can change settings for a desired email account that is stored on your Gear S2 as well as add a new email account to your smartwatch.

- » **Voice Memo:** If you record a voice memo on your Gear S2, the Voice Memo app transfers the voice memo to your smartphone automatically the next time your Gear S2 and smartphone are connected. You can transfer the voice memo only when you're charging your Gear S2, or you can turn off the automatic transfer entirely. However, you can transfer voice memos from the Gear S2 to your smartphone manually by tapping Transfer Now in the Voice Memo settings screen.

- » **Weather:** Add more cities for which you want weather information, and change the temperature measurement unit between Fahrenheit and Celsius. You can also set how often the Weather widget updates the weather condition for your area, from every hour to every 24 hours. You can also have the Gear S2 send or not send your current location to the Weather widget so that you can get weather information for your current area. (The default is to send your current location to the widget.)

Auto Update Downloaded Apps

By default, the Gear S2 downloads apps using Wi-Fi . Tap the Auto Update Downloaded Apps option to display a pop-up menu that shows three options. Via Wi-Fi Only is selected, as indicated by the orange text, but you can also use the carrier network for your Gear S2 (if your smartwatch is so equipped) by tapping Whenever Available. If you don't want to download apps to your Gear S2, tap Turn Off.

App Update Notifications

By default, your Gear S2 receives notifications about available updates for the apps you've downloaded to your smartwatch. If you don't want to receive these notifications, tap App Update Notifications, and the green slider with the green ON icon turns into a gray slider button and a gray OFF icon.

Double Press Home Key

This option allows you to change the app that opens when you double-press the Home button on your Gear S2. The default app is None. However, you can select from one of the following apps in the list (check Chapter 3 for a description of each of these apps):

» Last App

» Recent Apps

» Alarm

» Bloomberg

» Buddy

» CNN

» Email

» ESPN

» Find My Phone

» Gallery

» Maps

» Messages

» Music Player

» News Briefing

» Phone

» Nike+ Running

» S Health

» S Voice

» Samsung Milk Music

- » Schedule
- » Settings
- » Stopwatch
- » Timer
- » Voice Memo
- » Weather
- » World Clock

When you find an app you want, tap it. The Settings screen reappears, and you can see the app name underneath the Double Press Home Key entry in the list.

Gear Connection

Tap Gear Connection to open the Gear Connection screen. Within this screen, you can turn off the connection between the Gear S2 and your smartphone so that they can go their separate ways. (Did that make the Journey song pop in your head?) In the options list, you can turn off two options that are turned on by default:

- » **Remote connection:** When this option is turned on, you can use your Samsung account on your smartphone to connect to your Gear S2 remotely using Wi-Fi. If you turn this option off, you can't use the Notifications, Email, Messages, Find My Gear, or Find My Phone apps until your Gear S2 is connected to your smartphone using Bluetooth.
- » **Sync Wi-Fi profiles:** By default, your Gear S2 automatically connects to Wi-Fi networks saved on your phone. You can turn this option off by tapping Sync Wi-Fi Profiles in the list.

Return to the Settings screen by tapping the Back icon at the left side of the orange menu bar that appears at the top of the list.

Send SOS Messages

If you have a real emergency and need help, you may not be able to get to your smartphone, but having your watch on your wrist could make it possible to contact others. You can set up your Gear S2 to send an emergency message to as many as four people when you press the Home key quickly three times. That emergency message includes a note that says you're in an emergency situation and provides your current location. You can also attach a five-second audio recording when you send an emergency message.

There are several catches, of course:

>> You have to accept Samsung's terms and conditions, one of which is that your emergency message may not get through for some reason, such as there being no network connection.

>> You can't edit or even view the text message the Gear S2 sends to your contact(s).

>> Your Gear S2 needs to be connected to your smartphone to send SOS messages.

After you activate SOS messages, you can return the Settings screen by tapping the Back icon at the left side of the orange menu bar that appears at the top of the screen.

Back Up and Restore

You can back up settings data to your smartphone by tapping Back Up and Restore and then, in the screen that appears, tapping Back Up Data. If you've endured a freak mishap and have to reset your Gear S2, you can restore your backed-up settings by opening the Back Up and Restore screen in the Gear Manager app and then tapping Restore Data.

Return to the Settings screen (tap the Back icon), swipe up on the screen, and view the last two Settings options, which fall under the System section, as shown in Figure 4-6.

About Gear

Tap About Gear in the list to get interesting information and change a couple of important settings:

>> **Save Battery Power:** Learn how to save battery power on your Gear S2 such as by decreasing the screen brightness. You can also use power saving features on your Gear S2 that you can read about in Chapter 3.

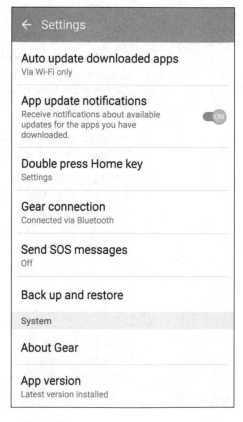

FIGURE 4-6:
The About Gear and App Version setting options appear in the System section.

- **>> Update Gear Software:** Check for updates to the smartwatch's Tizen operating system.

- **>> Gear Storage:** Find out how much storage is available on your Gear S2 and what apps are taking up your existing storage space.

- **>> Legal Information:** Read breathtaking legal information including the open source license, Samsung legalese, and the privacy notice for S Voice and voice-related functions.

- **>> Unknown Sources:** If you want to download and install Gear S2 apps from websites other than Samsung, tap Unknown Sources.

- **>> Device Name:** View the current device name in case someone (such as Samsung technical support) needs it.

You can return to the Settings screen by tapping the Back icon at the left side of the orange menu bar.

App Version

View the current version of the Gear S2 as well as the Gear Plug-in, which is the key component needed for Gear Manager to run. Go back to the Settings screen by tapping the Back icon in the orange menu bar.

Return to the main screen by (yes, again) tapping the Back icon at the left side of the orange menu bar (refer to Figure 4-6). Now you're back in the main Gear S2 screen.

Choosing how you want to be notified

Notifications are nice, but they can also be annoying if you keep getting a notification every few seconds. You can change the notifications that appear on your Gear S2 while you're wearing it by tapping Notifications. In the Notifications screen, you can turn notifications off completely by tapping On at the top of the screen shown in Figure 4-7.

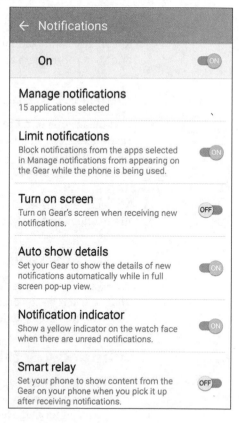

FIGURE 4-7:
The ON icon appears just below the orange menu bar at the top of the screen.

After you tap On, the green slider and green ON slider change to a gray slider and a gray OFF slider, and the rest of the options on the screen are disabled. If you keep notifications on, you can change five different notification settings.

Manage Notifications

When you tap Manage Notifications in the list, you see the Notifications screen that you saw when you first set up your Galaxy S2. I cover changing notifications in Chapter 2, but here's a quick recap: Swipe up and down to view all the apps on the Gear S2 that will give you notifications on your smartwatch. You can turn off notifications for an app by tapping the check box to the left of the selected app icon; when you do so, the check box turns white. If you want to turn on notifications for an app, tap the white check box to turn the check box green and add the white check mark.

If you prefer to receive notifications from all your apps, tap the All check box at the left side of the orange menu bar that appears at the top of the screen. When you're finished, tap Done at the right side of the menu bar.

Are you itching to learn more about notifications? You don't have to wait, you know. You can bookmark this page, go to Chapter 5, read all about notifications, and then return here all ready to learn how to you can limit notifications.

Limit Notifications

If you have one or more notifications from apps you selected in the Manage Notifications screen, the Gear S2 will prevent those app notifications from appearing on the smartwatch when your smartphone screen is on. However, you will still receive alarms on your Gear S2 when your smartphone screen is on.

You can turn off this feature by tapping Limit Notifications. When you do so, the green slider and green ON icon change to a gray slider and gray OFF icon.

Turn On Screen

When you receive a new notification, the Gear S2 screen doesn't come on. If you want the screen to come on, tap Turn On Screen to turn the gray slider and gray OFF icon to a green slider and green ON icon.

Auto Show Details

By default, the Gear S2 screen shows the details for notifications when you receive them. If you want to view only the title of the notification, tap Auto Show Details; the green slider and green ON slider change to a gray slider and green OFF icon.

Smart Relay

If you want to read your Gear S2 notifications on your smartphone, tap Smart Relay to change the gray slider and gray OFF icon to a green slider and green ON icon. The Smart Relay feature works only if your Gear S2 screen is on and the smartphone is unlocked.

REMEMBER

Some smartphones don't support the Smart Relay feature. If you're not sure whether your smartphone supports Smart Relay, contact either your smartphone manufacturer or Samsung at 1-800-SAMSUNG (that's 1-800-726-7864) to talk with a customer service representative and find out how well the Gear S2 plays with your smartphone.

Return to the main screen by tapping the Back icon at the left side of the orange menu bar that appears at the top of the screen.

Keeping Your Apps Up-to-Date

Reorder apps or delete one or more apps on your Gear S2 by tapping Apps Layout in the menu (refer to Figure 4-3). View how the app icons on each of the three app screens on the Gear S2 by swiping to the left and right in the app screen area below the orange menu bar shown in Figure 4-8.

The apps appear in order as they appear on the Gear S2 Apps screen when you swipe from right to left. In screen 1, Recent Apps starts at about the 1 o'clock position, the Messages app appears to the lower right of the Recent Apps icon, and so on.

Swipe up and down the list to view all the apps installed on your Gear S2. Move an app by tapping and holding the Move icon to the right of the app name (it looks like an up and down arrow) and then moving the app tile up to the appropriate location in the

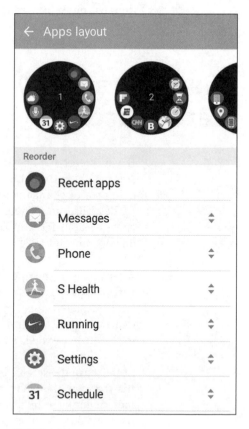

FIGURE 4-8:
Swipe from right to left to view the third Apps screen on your Gear S2.

list. An app tile contains the app icon, the app name, and the up and down arrow. Each tile is separated by a horizontal line.

As you move the app up and down, other app tiles in the list move up and down to make room for your selected app tile.

When you release your finger, the app tile appears in the new location in the list and the app tile also appears in its new location in the Gear S2 app screen above the list. For example, if you move the Gallery app in the list above S Voice, the Gallery and S Voice icons switch options in screen 1, which appears above the list.

If you move an app from one screen to another, the last app on the screen will be pushed to the next screen. For example, if you move the Weather app icon from screen 2 to screen 1, as shown in Figure 4-8, the last icon on screen 1 (the Gallery icon that's at about the 10 o'clock position) will move to screen 2 and take the place of the Weather icon. Neat.

Changing and Stylizing Watch Faces

If you prefer not to stare at a little screen (and perhaps hunch over while doing so) to change your watch face, as described in Chapter 3, you can change watch faces in Gear Manager on your smartphone.

After you open the Apps screen, navigate to the page that contains the Gear Manager app, and then start Gear Manager. Now tap Watch Faces in the menu as you see in Figure 4-9.

At the top of the screen, you see a large tile that contains your current watch face, and it even tells you the current time and date without your having to look at or turn on the Gear S2.

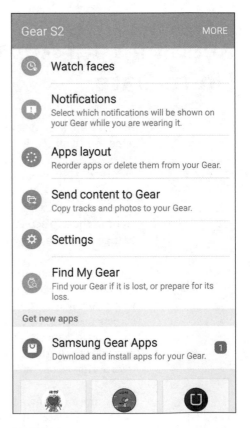

FIGURE 4-9:
The Watch Faces menu option appears near the top of the screen directly underneath the orange menu bar.

Changing your face from your smartphone

Smaller tiles appear underneath the current watch face tile so that you can see all the faces you can choose from by swiping up and down in the screen. The Modern Utility tile text underneath the watch face is highlighted in orange (see Figure 4-10), indicating that this is the selected face.

When you find a face you like, just tap the tile. The current watch face tile changes to show your new face; also, the text in the tile you selected changes to orange and you see the watch face on your Gear S2 screen.

As you swipe up to go to the bottom of the tile list, the current watch face tile doesn't move. If you don't find a watch tile you like, you can shop for a new face in the Samsung Galaxy Apps store by tapping the Add Template icon, as shown in Figure 4-11.

FIGURE 4-10:
The Modern Utility tile text is orange and includes an example of what the face looks like.

FIGURE 4-11:
The Add Template icon is an orange plus sign.

The Add Template screen, shown in Figure 4-12, displays a list of watch faces that you can add to your Gear S2. In this example, you have six watch faces to choose from, but they are all installed on your Gear S2 already. You can return to the watch faces screen by tapping the Back icon in the orange menu bar.

You can view three featured faces at the bottom of the screen within the Featured section (refer to Figure 4-11). Tap a tile to view the details about the face and how much it costs (if anything) in the Galaxy Apps store.

If those featured faces don't float your boat, tap More to open a list of watch faces in the Samsung Galaxy Apps screen, shown in Figure 4-13. Swipe up and down the screen to view all the faces. Each tile tells you the name of the face and shows a thumbnail image or logo as well as the price of the face. If the watch face is already installed, you see Installed within the tile instead of a price.

Tap the tile to learn more about the face as well as to purchase or download the face in the Details screen. If you change your mind, just tap the Back icon in the upper-left corner of the screen to return to the Gear > Watch Faces screen. Return safe and sound to the Gear Manager screen by tapping the Back button in the upper-left corner of the Gear > Watch Faces screen.

Stylizing your face

Now you're ready to stylize your watch face to change the look of the

FIGURE 4-12:
The Back icon is at the left end of the orange menu bar that appears at the top of the screen.

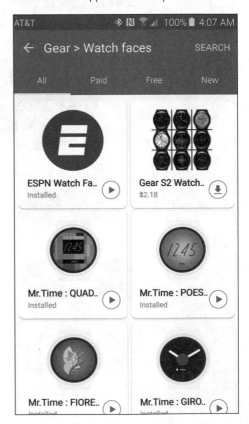

FIGURE 4-13:
Swipe up and down in the screen to see the wide selection of watch faces to choose from.

dial, hands, and more. Start by tapping Stylize at the lower right of the selected face tile, as shown in Figure 4-14.

Below the selected face tile, you see a gray bar that contains alternative watch faces you can select (see Figure 4-15). Swipe back and forth to view all the alternative faces. If you find one you like, tap it. The current watch face at the top of the screen changes to match the face you selected.

If you want to stylize specific parts of the watch face you selected, you do that in the Dial section, which appears underneath the bar and shows several dial styles. Swipe up and down the screen to view all the dial styles, as shown in Figure 4-16. When you find one you like, tap the dial. The current watch face at the top of the screen changes to match the face you selected.

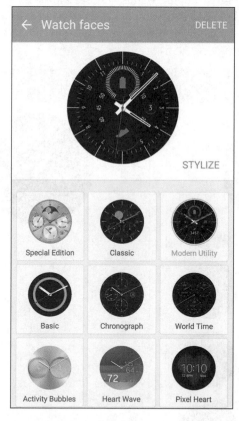

FIGURE 4-14:
The selected face tile appears in the upper third of the screen, just below the orange menu bar.

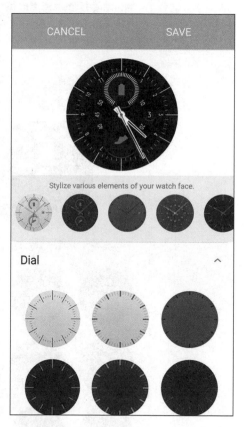

FIGURE 4-15:
Swipe left and right within the gray bar to view all the face styles you can choose from.

Swipe down to the bottom of the screen to view the other Watch Face setting categories as well as the Show Date setting. The number of settings categories you see depends on the watch face you're editing. For the Modern Utility face, you find three different categories: Hands, Complication 1, which by default is Battery, and Complication 2, which by default are the number of steps you've taken since you turned the watch on.

TECHNICAL STUFF

Horology is defined as both the study of time as well as clocks and watches. In horology speak, a *complication* is a feature in a timepiece that goes beyond the display of hours and minutes. A complication can be as something as common as a date or something as unique as the current battery strength level on your Gear S2.

The styles under each category are hidden, but you can show all the hand styles by tapping Hands in the list. After tapping Hands, you see all the hand styles, shown in Figure 4-17. Tap one of the hand styles to apply the style to your face within the selected face tile. You can hide all the hand styles by tapping the Hands category name.

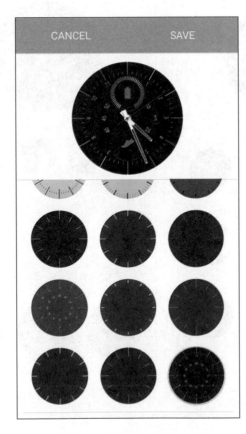

FIGURE 4-16:
The selected face tile doesn't move when you swipe up and down the screen to view all the dial styles.

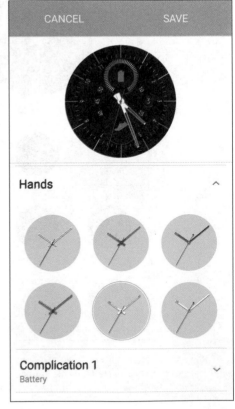

FIGURE 4-17:
You can select from one of six hand styles within the Hands category.

Tap Complication 1 to change what you see in place of the battery and then swipe up the screen to view all 14 options (see Figure 4-18).

The default for the Modern Utility face is the battery icon that has a semicircle around it. Small white lines appear within the semicircle when the battery is full. When you start losing battery power, the white lines at the right side of the semicircle turn gray. As you lose more power, lines turn gray in a counterclockwise motion around the semicircle.

If you prefer a more direct representation of your battery life, you can show the battery percentage level from 0 (empty) to 100 (full). If you don't want to see the battery, you can tap the Weather icon to instead show the current weather temperature and sky condition for your location, or tap the Heart Rate icon to display your current heart rate. You don't have to show anything, either: Just tap None. As you tap each option, you see the changes to your face within the selected face tile.

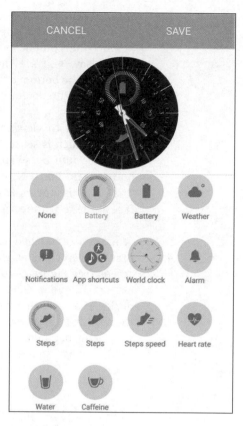

FIGURE 4-18:
All 14 options within the Complication 1 category.

You can hide the Complication 1 options by swiping down the screen and then tapping the Complication 1 category name. Now tap Complication 2 to view all options in that category. The Steps option appears by default, enabling you to see the number of steps (look at the bottom of the watch face) that you've taken since you turned on the watch.

Swipe up and down to view all 14 options, as shown in Figure 4-19. You can show nothing by tapping None or show how much caffeine you've recorded as having ingested in terms of cups of coffee by tapping Caffeine. (Or any of the others in between.)

You hide the Complication 2 options by swiping up the screen and then tapping the Complication 2 category name. Now you see the Show Date setting at the bottom of the screen, as shown in Figure 4-20.

Swipe down to view the Show Date setting, which is set to On by default. Hide the date by swiping the slider button from left (ON) to right (OFF). The date disappears from the watch face at the top of the screen.

When you're finished, tap Save in the orange menu bar at the top of the screen (see Figure 4-20) to apply the changes to your watch face. If you decide that you like the watch face the way it is after all, tap Cancel in the menu bar and then tap Discard in the Leave Stylize Screen pop-up window.

Rubbing out a face

If you don't want a face taking up valuable storage space on your Gear S2, you can go to your smartwatch to remove the face, as described in Chapter 3, or you can delete a face within the Gear Manager app by tapping Delete at the right side of the orange menu bar (see Figure 4-21).

Now all but one of the face tiles appear with a Delete icon in the upper-right area of the tile, as shown in Figure 4-22. You can't delete your currently selected face, which in Figure 4-22 is the Modern Utility face, because you need a watch face for your Gear S2 to work.

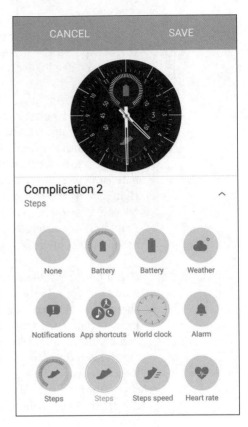

FIGURE 4-19:
The Steps icon circle is outlined in orange and the Steps text is in orange, indicating that this feature is selected.

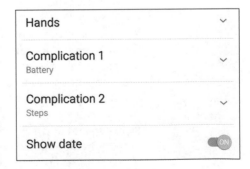

FIGURE 4-20:
The Show Date option is at the bottom of the screen.

FIGURE 4-21:
The orange menu bar appears at the top of the screen above the selected face tile.

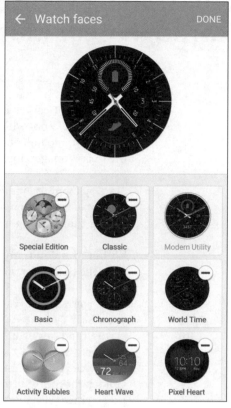

FIGURE 4-22:
The Delete icon in each tile is a red minus sign inside a white circle.

Swipe up and down the screen to view all the faces that you can delete. When you find the face, tap the Delete icon within the face tile. In the Remove pop-up window, delete the watch face by tapping OK. If you change your mind, tap Cancel.

When you're finished deleting watch faces, tap Done at the right side of the orange menu bar (refer to Figure 4-22). Within that same orange menu bar, tap the Back icon at the left side of the menu bar to return to the main Gear Manager screen.

Controlling Your Gear S2 through Gear Manager

Your Gear S2 can't sprout legs and walk away, but it can be misplaced. Before you start searching under couch cushions and in drawers, find your charger to see whether the Gear S2 is docked and thus hiding in plain sight. If you confirm that the Gear S2 is not with its charger, or you don't have your charger with you, it's time for you to pull out your smartphone and find your wayward smartwatch with the Gear Manager app.

Start by tapping Find My Gear in the Gear Manager screen on your smartphone, shown in Figure 4-23.

Within the Find My Gear screen, start the search for your gear by tapping the Start icon. Under the Start icon, you see the current status of your Gear S2 battery, its connection status, and an icon that indicates whether the Gear S2 screen is locked or unlocked (see Figure 4-24). After you tap the Start button, which is the green circle with a white magnifying glass inside it, the Gear S2 vibrates and the screen is turned on so that you can both hear and look for your smartwatch.

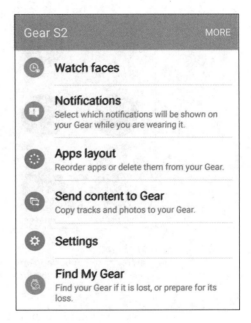

FIGURE 4-23:
The Find My Gear option is the only one that has a green icon.

Locking your Gear S2

If you don't want someone to access your Gear S2 when you don't have it on, tap Reactivation Lock at the top of the screen (refer to Figure 4-24). In the Reactivation Lock screen, shown in Figure 4-25, tap Off to turn Reactivation Lock on.

The Samsung Account window appears on the screen so that you can add your Samsung account. If you don't have a Samsung account, you see a window that prompts you to add an account. If you don't want a Samsung account, you won't be able to lock your Gear S2 from your smartphone. It's that simple.

If you already have a Samsung account, as in this example, type the password into the Confirm Password field. Then tap Confirm. After a few seconds, the gray slider and gray OFF button in the Reactivation Lock screen change to a green slider and green ON button. Now you can return to the Find My Gear screen by tapping the Back icon at the left side of the orange menu bar.

TIP

If you take the time to read the text on the Reactivation Lock screen, you notice that if you contact Samsung to have your Gear S2 repaired via warranty, you need to turn off Reactivation Lock so that the nice tech support people can get access to your smartwatch and find out what's happening.

Controlling your Gear S2 remotely

If your smartphone and Gear S2 are both connected to a Wi-Fi or data carrier network (that is, not connected to each other with Bluetooth), you can control the Gear S2 remotely to lock the smartwatch. What's more, you can reset your Gear S2 from the Gear Manager app.

In the Find My Gear screen, shown previously in Figure 4-24, tap Control Remotely in the list. Within the Control Remotely screen shown in Figure 4-26, you can lock your Gear S2 by tapping Lock Gear or reset the Gear S2 by tapping Reset Gear.

Locking and unlocking your Gear S2

If you're not sure whether your Gear S2 and smartwatch are connected via Bluetooth, tap Lock Gear. If your phone and watch are connected, a

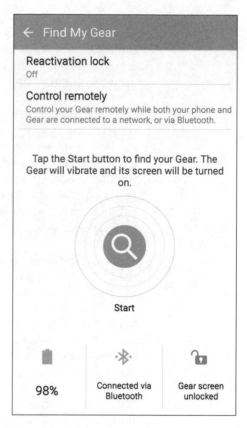

FIGURE 4-24:
The Start button appears in the center of the screen.

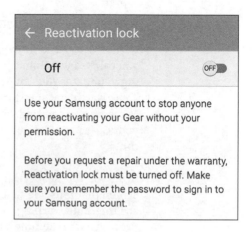

FIGURE 4-25:
The Off option appears just below the orange menu bar at the top of the screen.

pop-up message appears on your smartphone screen that says you can't lock the Gear S2 while your smartphone and smartwatch are connected with Bluetooth.

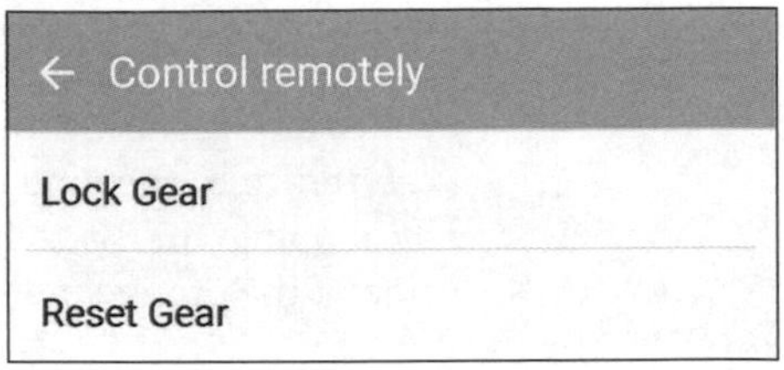

After you turn off Bluetooth on the Gear S2, the Find My Gear option in the Gear Manager app is disabled for a few seconds as the app determines whether your Gear S2 is connected to a Wi-Fi or data carrier network. After the app is satisfied that the Gear S2 is connected to such a network, the Find My Gear option is active, which means that you can open the Control Remotely screen and then tap Lock Gear.

The Lock Gear screen appears, tell you about what Lock Gear does and warning that the Lock Gear feature may take some time to function or may not work, depending on the state of your Gear S2, your smartphone, or your mobile environment.

Tap OK at the bottom right of the screen to lock your Gear S2. After a second or two, a pop-up menu appears at the bottom of the screen informing you that the Gear is locked. It's that easy. A few seconds after that, you return to the Gear Manager home screen.

Unlocking your Gear S2 is even easier. When you pick up the smartwatch, you see the Gear Locked icon for a couple of seconds. Then you see the watch face showing the time again. Your Gear S2 is unlocked and its Bluetooth connection with your smartphone is restored.

Resetting your Gear S2

If your Gear S2 is in the clutches of villains and the Scooby gang isn't available, you can use your smartphone to reset your Gear S2 and keep others from accessing your data. You can perform this reset from your smartphone only if both your smartwatch and smartphone are connected through a Wi-Fi network and the Gear Manager app can find your phone. You can also use the Gear Manager app to reset your Gear S2 using a Bluetooth connection if resetting on your smartphone is your thing.

After you tap Reset Gear in the Control Remotely options list, you see a warning screen that tells you that all data on the Gear S2 will be deleted. What's more, you see the same warning as you find on the Lock Gear feature, saying that the reset process may take time or even fail to function.

FIGURE 4-26:
Use this screen to lock or reset your Gear S2.

If you want to continue with the reset, tap OK. The Samsung Account window opens, and you need to type your Samsung account password and then tap Confirm. The Gear Manager app disconnects from your Gear S2 and closes, and the Gear S2 screen states that a factory reset is in progress.

When the reset is complete, you see a Bluetooth pairing request from the Gear S2 on your smartphone. After you tap OK to accept the request, look at your Gear S2 screen and tap the Confirm button on the right side of the Confirm Passkey screen. The Gear Manager app starts again and asks you to connect to your Gear S2. Connect Gear Manager to your Gear S2 by tapping OK in the Warning pop-up window.

After your Gear S2 is back on your wrist safe and sound, you can try to restore any backed-up data to your smartwatch. If there is any data to restore to your Gear S2, you see the Restore screen on your smartphone (see Figure 4-27) that tells you what you can restore, such as settings. You can skip restoration by tapping the Restore check box; the check box changes from a green background with a white check mark to just a plain white background. For this example, I want to restore my settings, so I leave the check box alone and click Next.

It takes a little while for your smartphone to restore your data, but when it's done, the Terms and Conditions screen appears, which is the first step in setting up your Gear S2. Accepting terms and conditions is a quick, three-step process:

1. **Tap the Agree to Terms of the End User License Agreement check box.**

2. **Tap the Agree to All check box.**

3. **Tap Done.**

FIGURE 4-27:
The Restore check box appears in the lower-left corner of the screen.

Now you see the Sign In to Samsung Account screen, which shows that the reactivation lock is on for your Gear S2. This means that you need to sign in to your Samsung account to confirm that the Gear S2 is actually yours. By default, the

Keep Reactivation Lock On After Setup check box is selected, and you can leave that as is and tap Sign In.

The Samsung Account window appears on the screen so that you can enter your password. (If you don't have a Samsung account, you see a screen that starts you on the path to creating one.) After you type your password, tap Confirm in the window. After a second or two, the Gear Manager app home screen appears, your Gear S2 data is restored, and all is right with the world again.

2

Places You Can Go on Gear S2

IN THIS PART . . .

Creating, reviewing, and customizing notifications on your Gear S2

Using your Gear S2 with your smartphone to make and get calls, texts, and emails

Listening to your favorite music with the built-in Music app

Talking to your Gear S2 using the S Voice app

Monitoring and improving your health with the S Health app

Chapter 5

Getting Notified: An Alarm Watch on Steroids

Y ou can buy an analog or digital alarm watch at many different online and brick-and-mortar stores, so it's no surprise that you can set an alarm on your Gear S2 that alerts you about an upcoming event or even wakes you up from a well-deserved nap.

But your Gear S2 goes much farther (which is why you have one). You can view notifications from your phone, such as a new email message, as well as view information about upcoming appointments in the Schedule app. And you can use — and add — a wide variety of widgets to get the most from your Gear S2 Even your skeptical friends will be impressed.

In this chapter, you start by learning how to review notifications you've received on your Gear S2. Then you find out how to locate preinstalled widgets as well as add widgets to your smartwatch. Finally, the chapter shows you how to schedule an appointment on your smartphone and view that appointment on your Gear S2.

Reviewing Your Notifications

When you receive a notification, you see the text of the notification on the Gear S2 screen, as shown in Figure 5-1. You can then decide whether you want to have the notification occur again in a bit by tapping the Snooze icon on the right side of the screen or dismiss it altogether by tapping the Dismiss icon.

You can also press the Home button to go back to the watch screen without dismissing the notification or putting it on snooze. When you do, you see an orange dot over the 9 o'clock marker (see Figure 5-2). The orange dot tells you that you have one or more active notifications that need your attention.

FIGURE 5-1:
The gold Snooze icon is on the right; the red Dismiss icon is on the left.

View your notifications by swiping from left to right on the screen. The most recent notification text appears on the screen, as shown in Figure 5-3. Tap the notification text to open the app associated with the notification, such as the Email app if your notification is about an email message.

FIGURE 5-2:
The orange notification dot appears on the left side of the watch screen.

FIGURE 5-3:
The icon of the app that relates to your notification appears at the top of the screen.

If you have more than one new notification, the number of notifications appears at the bottom of the screen (refer to Figure 5-3). The first notification appears in the center of the screen (see Figure 5-4), and you can view all notifications by swiping up and down in the screen. Tap a notification to open the app associated with said notification.

If you want to go back to the watch screen without viewing any of the notifications, press the Home button. Alas and alack, you can view the notifications only once. The next time you swipe left to right on the watch screen to view the Notifications screen, you see either No Notifications or only any new notifications you've received since you returned to the watch screen.

FIGURE 5-4:
Tap View All at the top of the screen to view all the email messages.

Reviewing and Adding Widgets

Your Gear S2 comes chock-full of widgets that you can use to get notifications about what's going on in your world right on your wrist. Several widgets require you to connect with your smartphone to work correctly. For example, the Weather widget on your Gear S2 needs to use the GPS functionality on your smartphone to find your current location and give you an accurate weather report.

Viewing widgets

You can easily view widgets: Just swipe from right to left on the watch screen to view each of the nine preinstalled widgets. The following sections describe the widgets that appear in order as you swipe from right to left.

Weather

The Weather widget shows you the current conditions for your current location, including an icon for the current sky condition, the current temperature, and the high and low temperatures forecasted for the day (see Figure 5-5).

Tap the Weather widget screen to get more information. You can also swipe from right to left to open the Add City screen and then add a city by tapping the Add City icon. After you add a city, you can view that city's current weather conditions by tapping the Weather widget and swiping from right to left on the screen.

Daily Schedule

You're a busy person, and the Daily Schedule widget is here to help by showing you a list of all your appointments for the day. Tap the Daily Schedule screen shown in Figure 5-6 to swipe up and down the appointments screen and view your appointments for the rest of the day as well as the rest of the month.

If you don't have any appointments for the day, you instead see the weather forecast for your location. Tap the widget screen to view all your upcoming appointments for the month.

Steps

The Steps widget, shown in Figure 5-7, automatically tracks the number of steps you've taken since you turned the watch on and have worn it on your wrist. Tap the widget to show how many steps you've taken toward your daily goal — or just to get an eye-opening reminder of how many steps you actually take every day.

FIGURE 5-5:
The current time appears at the top of the Weather widget screen.

FIGURE 5-6:
The current date and day of the week appear at the top of the Daily Schedule screen.

Heart Rate Tracker

If you want to see your current pulse as you move, tap the Heart Rate Tracker widget icon, shown in Figure 5-8, so the widget can measure your pulse for the first time. Tapping the widget icon activates the scanners on the back side of the watch case that sense your pulse, and after a few seconds, you see your pulse rate in beats per minute.

The next time you open the Heart Rate Tracker widget, you see the pulse you had the last time you used the widget and how long ago the widget took your pulse. Tap the widget to take your current pulse.

FIGURE 5-7:
If you haven't taken any steps since you turned on the Gear S2, the number of steps recorded is 0.

Flipboard News

The Flipboard News widget shows you the top two stories aggregated from leading national news organizations (see Figure 5-9). Tap one of the story titles to view the story list screen.

FIGURE 5-8:
The Heart Rate Tracker widget screen asks you to set up the tracker and measure your pulse for the first time.

FIGURE 5-9:
The number of new stories in your Flipboard newsfeed appears at the bottom of the screen (in this case, 10).

Swipe up and down in this screen to view 12 different story titles in a variety of categories, including the two top stories you viewed in the first widget screen. Within the story list screen, tap a story name to read the story on the screen.

World Clock: Add City

You can see the time for another city that you may be traveling to soon, or that a special someone is currently visiting, using the World Clock widget. Here's how to view time for a city within the widget:

1. **In the watch screen, swipe from right to left until you see the World Clock widget, shown in Figure 5-10.**

2. **Tap the Add City icon in the World Clock widget screen.**

3. **Swipe back and forth within the world map until the overlapping light white vertical bar is over the area where you want the time.**

   A list of cities in that selected area, including the current time, appears in the transparent icon in the bottom third of the screen.

4. **Tap the icon to place the city and time within the World Clock widget screen.**

   The city and time appear on the screen. You can change them by tapping the screen and swiping left and right on the map to find a new area.

FIGURE 5-10:
Tap the screen to add a city.

Start Workout

If you run to stay fit, you can start monitoring a 30-minute running workout by tapping the Start Workout widget screen, shown in Figure 5-11. You begin a three-second countdown and then see the timer on the screen that shows how long you've run and your current pulse. The widget uses the accelerometer and gyroscope built into your Gear S2 to track your speed and movement. It then converts that information into the length of your run and more useful information that's easy to get.

Just rotate the bezel to the right (or swipe from right to left on the screen) to view the distance you've run, the number of calories you've burned, your current pace, your current speed, and your heart rate. Tap any screen in the widget to view the current time and to pause the run by tapping the Pause icon at the bottom of the screen.

Music

Need to get your groove on fast? The Music widget makes it easy to play the current song in your playlist within the Music Player app on your Gear S2. (You learn more about the Music Player in Chapter 7.) Here's how:

FIGURE 5-11:
Start the three-second countdown to your 30-minute workout by tapping the screen.

1. **In the watch screen, swipe from right to left until you see the Music widget, shown in Figure 5-12.**

2. **Tap the Play icon in the center of the screen.**

   The title of the song appears under the Play icon and the song starts playing either on your smartphone or your Bluetooth headset.

3. **Tap the Play Next icon to the right of the Play icon to play the next song in your playlist.**

4. **Tap the Previous icon to the left of the Play icon to play the previous song in your playlist.**

FIGURE 5-12:
Open the Music app to manage your music by tapping Open App at the bottom of the screen.

Add Widget

You can add another widget by swiping from right to left on the screen through the widgets list until you see the Add Widget screen, shown in Figure 5-13. After you tap the icon, the Add Widget screen appears with seven more widgets to choose from, as you see in the next section.

TIP

To go back to another widget, just swipe left to right on the screen. Eventually you return to the watch screen, but you can save yourself some time and your finger some effort by just pressing the Home button.

FIGURE 5-13:
The Add Widget icon looks like a plus sign.

Selecting a widget to add

Although more widgets are already "preinstalled," they're not part of the widgets list. You can access one or more of these hidden widgets by opening the Add Widget screen and then adding a widget to the list.

Start by swiping from right to left in the watch screen until you see the Add Widget screen. Tap the Add Widget icon (refer to Figure 5-13). In the Add Widget screen, swipe from right to left to view all eight widgets you can add. The last two widgets are the Weather and World Clock widgets, but you don't need to worry about these because they're already accessible within the widgets list.

Alarm

You tap the Alarm widget, shown in Figure 5-14, to add a new alarm. (I go into the details of adding an alarm learn to do later in this chapter, in "Setting and Deleting an Alarm.") If you already have an alarm set up, this widget shows you the date and time of your next alarm.

FIGURE 5-14:
The Alarm widget image shows you an example of what an alarm looks like on the screen.

App Shortcuts

The App Shortcuts widget, shown in Figure 5-15, is a great way to access features that you may use more often than others on your Gear S2. Samsung has decided that you'll probably want to use four shortcuts that appear as icons within the widget in clockwise order: Apps, Buddy, Settings, and S Voice.

The Apps icon opens the Apps screen, of course. The Buddy app is a list of your favorite contacts that you can access to quickly call or send a text message to a favorite person. The Settings icon opens the Settings screen, and the S Voice app allows you to talk to your Galaxy S2. I cover how to use S Voice in detail in Chapter 8.

FIGURE 5-15:
The App Shortcuts widget contains four app icons.

S Health Activity Log

The S Health Activity Log widget gives you a quick look at your activities of the past 24 hours. As Figure 5-16 shows, you see color-coded bands within the circle around the perimeter of the screen. The three bands represent healthy (green), light activity (yellow), and inactivity (white). This information tells you how you spend your day so that you can figure out whether you need to exercise more to stay fit.

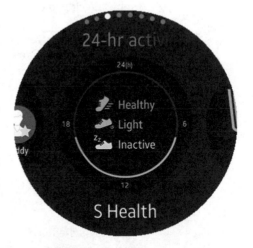

FIGURE 5-16:
The S Health activity log image shows you the icons for healthy, light, and inactive activity levels.

S Health Water and Caffeine

We can't survive without water, and many of us feel as though we can't survive without caffeine, either. However, you need to get the right balance of water to caffeine, and the S Health Water and Caffeine widget helps you do just that. After you add this widget, you can tap the plus icon underneath the water glass (blue) and caffeinated beverage cups (brown; see Figure 5-17) as you consume these beverages. If you aren't feeling well throughout the day, perhaps you should change your balance of water to caffeine and see whether that change helps you feel better.

Samsung Milk Music

Samsung Milk Music is Samsung's streaming music service, which selects a few songs in many musical categories so that you can listen to music throughout the day. You can also listen to sports radio stations.

FIGURE 5-17:
The Water and Caffeine widget shows the glasses of water versus caffeinated beverages that you've tracked.

Samsung gives you Milk Music in two forms on your Gear S2. The first is the full-fledged app that lets you select songs to listen to in a category as well as listen to those songs individually. The other form is the Samsung Milk Music widget, which lets you start listening to those songs quickly without having to wade through the Apps screen.

After you set up the Milk Music app, as I cover in detail in Chapter 7, you can add this widget (see Figure 5-18) to your Gear S2 so that you can access music in your preferred category more easily.

Schedule

Earlier in this chapter, I tell you about the Daily Schedule widget, which lists your appointments for the current day. The Gear S2 offers a different widget, called Schedule (see Figure 5-19), which that lets you view the monthly calendar. As with the Daily Schedule widget, when you tap the Schedule widget screen, you see the list of appointments and events (such as holidays) over the next month.

With the Schedule widget, you tap the month shown on the screen to view your entire list of events for the rest of that month starting from the current date. I show you how to add this and other widgets shortly.

FIGURE 5-18:
You need to set up Milk Music on your Gear S2 before you can add the widget.

FIGURE 5-19:
The Schedule widget shows you the current month; the current date appears within a green circle.

Adding a widget

The previous sections in this chapter take you on a tour of all the widgets. Here's a quick primer to show how you add any of those widgets.

1. **In the watch screen, swipe from right to left until you see the Add Widget icon.**

2. **Tap the Add Widget icon.**

3. **In the Add Widget screen, swipe from right to left in the screen until you see the widget you want to add.**

4. **Tap the widget to add it.**

   The widget icon appears in between the Music Player and Add Widget widgets (see Figure 5-20). Now tap the icon to add the widget to the widget list. The widget now appears on the screen, and you can access it anytime you want.

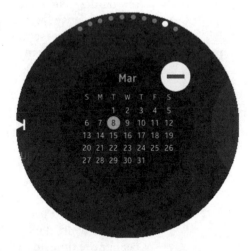

FIGURE 5-20:
The widget icon appears in the center of the screen.

TIP

If you add a widget but decide that you don't like it, you can delete it from the widgets list:

1. **On the watch screen, swipe right to left until you see the widget you don't want.**

2. **Tap and hold the screen until you see the widget screen with the Delete icon (refer to Figure 5-20).**

3. **Tap the Delete icon.**

   The widget goes away. Nothing to it. After you delete the widget from the list, you can add it to the list again from the Add Widgets screen.

Setting and Deleting an Alarm

Fun fact: The first wrist watch with an alarm was produced by the Swiss watchmaker Eterna all the way back in 1914. Today you can find plenty of wrist watches with alarms, and even though your Gear S2 isn't a mechanical watch, the Alarm app comes preinstalled on your smartwatch so that you can set and hear alarms.

To set an alarm, press the Home button on the Gear S2 to open the Apps screen. Now swipe from right to left to move to the second page on the Apps screen, shown in Figure 5-21. Tap the Alarm icon.

The Alarm app screen looks the same as the Alarm widget. Tap the Add Alarm icon, shown in Figure 5-22, to start adding an alarm.

In the Set Time screen, shown in Figure 5-23, you can tell that the hour is selected because it's blinking blue and white. Follow these steps to change the time on the screen:

FIGURE 5-21:
The Alarm icon appears at about the 2 o'clock position on the screen.

1. **Rotate the bezel right and left to change the hour.**

2. **Tap the minute number to make it blink in blue and white.**

3. **Rotate the bezel left and right to change the minute.**

4. **Tap AM to change the time of day to PM, if appropriate.**

   If you want to change the time of day back to AM, tap PM.

5. **Tap the Next icon.**

   The Repeat Weekly screen appears, as shown in Figure 5-24. The days of the week from Sunday through Wednesday appear in the top row, and Thursday through Saturday appear in the bottom row.

6. **Tap the icon with the day of the current week when you want to hear the alarm.**

   If you want the alarm to repeat more than once during the week, tap one or more days in the week as appropriate. If you want to hear the alarm at the same time every day of the week, tap each icon on the screen.

   As you tap a day, the circle for that day turns from an outlined hollow circle to a solid blue circle.

7. **Tap Save.**

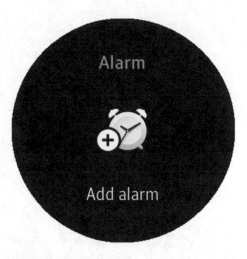

FIGURE 5-22:
The Add Alarm icon appears in the center of the screen.

FIGURE 5-23:
The blue Next icon appears at the bottom of the screen.

FIGURE 5-24:
The red S denotes Sunday.

Your next alarm appears on the Alarm screen (see Figure 5-25).

8. **Add another alarm by tapping Add at the bottom of the screen.**

If you've set more than one alarm, the most recent alarm that you added appears in the center of the Alarm screen. You can view more alarms and add another alarm by swiping up in the Alarm screen.

TIP

To delete an alarm, just tap and hold your finger on the alarm until a green check mark appears in the middle of the alarm entry. Swipe up and down the screen and tap another alarm if

FIGURE 5-25:
The Add icon.

you want to delete multiple alarms. When you're done, tap Delete at the bottom of the screen. The Alarm screen shows your remaining alarms or the Add Alarm icon if you deleted all your alarms.

Scheduling Your Busy Life

The Schedule app on your Gear S2, described briefly earlier in this chapter, can access your schedule from the Calendar app on your smartphone as well as let you create an event on your smartphone that your Gear S2 will automatically add to the Schedule app. (They don't call it a smartwatch for nothing.)

The Gear S2 doesn't have enough storage space to store your schedule. So, because your smartwatch works with your smartphone to complete various tasks, such as making a call if your Gear S2 doesn't have 3G connectivity, the Gear S2 stores your schedule on your smartphone. But that setup also makes life easier for you because your schedule on both your smartphone and your Gear S2 are synced automatically.

To open the Schedule app on your Gear S2, press the Home button. Next, tap the Schedule icon within the first page of the Apps screen, shown in Figure 5-26. If you're looking at a different page within the Apps screen, swipe from left to right on the screen to get to the first page.

Viewing events

When you open the Schedule app on your Gear S2, you see the current month (see Figure 5-27). You can swipe up and down on the screen to view your calendar one month at a time, starting with your current month.

FIGURE 5-26:
The Schedule app icon appears at the 8 o'clock position on the screen.

FIGURE 5-27:
The current month includes the current date within a green circle.

REMEMBER

Unfortunately, you can view events only for the next 31 days on your Gear S2 (at least as of this writing). If you create an event beyond 31 days from your current date, you won't be able to see the event on your Gear S2 until that future month becomes the current month.

No matter what month you're looking at, you can view the current month by tapping once on the screen. Now that you can see your current month, tap the screen once to view your schedule. The first event on your day's schedule appears in the center of the screen, as shown in Figure 5-28. The current date appears above that event, and you can swipe up and down on the screen to view other events on the same or different days in the current month.

FIGURE 5-28:
The first event on your current day's schedule, which is the day's weather forecast, appears in the center of the screen.

Creating an Event

The process for creating an event isn't as streamlined as it could be because you can't create events right in the Schedule app on the Gear S2 (at least as of this writing). So you need to grab your smartphone and add an event on your smartphone's calendar app. For this example, I add an event in the Calendar app on my Samsung Galaxy S6.

On your smartphone, start by tapping the App icon on the Home screen to open the Apps screen. Then tap Calendar, as shown in Figure 5-29.

The calendar for the current month appears on the screen, and any events you add are included under the date. The current date is green and appears inside a green circle. To add an event in the current month, tap the green Add icon, shown in Figure 5-30.

FIGURE 5-29:
Tap the Calendar app icon.

FIGURE 5-30:
The Add icon appears in the lower-right corner of the screen.

The Add Event screen appears (see Figure 5-31). The Title field holds a blinking cursor, patiently waiting for you to type in the title of your event. After you type the title, follow these steps to start adding the event:

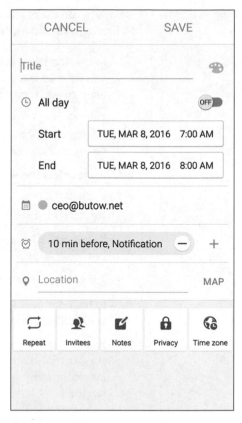

1. **Tap the palette icon to select an event color in the Select Event Color window.**

   You can use different event colors to differentiate between types of events in your calendar.

2. **Slide the All Day slider from left (OFF) to right (ON) if the event will happen all day.**

3. **Tap the date and time in the Start field to enter the start date and time of the event within the Set Date and Time window.**

   You can also use the controls in the window to designate an event for a future date. When you tap the date and time in the Start field, the Calendar window appears, allowing you to select a future date and time.

FIGURE 5-31:
The menu bar at the top of the screen contains the Cancel and Save options.

4. **Change the event date by swiping left and right within the calendar to view months and dates; then tap the date for the event within the calendar.**

5. **Tap the up- and down-arrows in the hour and minute tiles to enter the start time for the event.**

6. **Tap the time-of-day tile to change the time between AM and PM.**

7. **Tap Done when you've finished setting the Start date.**

8. **Tap the date and time in the End field to set the ending date and time for the event in the same way as you did with the start date and time.**

Next, you can make this event appear on the calendar as well as set up a reminder. Still using your smartphone, follow these steps:

1. **In the Add Event screen within the Calendar app, tap the email address if you want to change the account that contains the calendar to which you want to add the event.**

   The Calendar window opens, and you specify the account by tapping it in the list. You can choose from My Calendars, which is the calendar stored on the Galaxy S6, or another calendar, such as the one stored in your Google account.

2. **Right below the email address, tap the Reminder field.**

   The Reminder screen appears. The default reminder is 10 Min Before, Notification.

3. **Tap Notification in the upper-right corner of the screen to have the event reminder appear as a notification.**

   Alternatively, you can send the notification to your email account.

4. **In the Reminder screen list, tap the time before the event that you want the notification to appear on the screen.**

   You can select from five options ranging from On Time (the time the event starts) to one day before the start time. You can also customize the time interval by tapping Customize and then setting the time in the Reminder window.

   After you set the notification time, you return to the Add Event screen automatically and you see the notification time you selected in the Reminder field. You remove the notification, if you want, by tapping the red minus icon to the right of the alarm information.

5. **Tap the plus icon at the right of the Reminder field to add another notification, if you'd like, that will appear at a different time or be delivered in a different manner.**

Finally, add the location and other details that you might like to include for the event:

1. **Tap the Location field to type a location for the event.**

   If you want to find the location in the Maps app instead of typing it in, tap Map to the right of the Location field and find the location in the Google Maps app.

2. **Tap the tiles at the bottom of the screen (these appear from left to right):**

   - Repeat: You can sets a repeating cycle for the event.
   - Invitees: You can add names from your Contacts list.

- Notes: Type a description for the event.

- Privacy: Make the event viewable only by you. (Otherwise, the event is public, so anyone who sees your calendar can view the event.)

- Time Zone: You can change the time zone for the event.

3. **Tap Save at the top of the screen to complete the event and save it to your calendar.**

   If you decide that you don't want to add the event after all, tap Cancel.

Now the event appears in your calendar on your smartphone, and you can check to see the new event on your Gear S2. Here's what to do:

1. **Open the Schedule app on your Gear S2.**

2. **Tap the current month to view all the events for the month.**

3. **Swipe up until you see the event in your calendar.**

4. **Tap the event to view more information, including the event location.**

If your event has a time scheduled, such as from 10:00 a.m. to 6:00 p.m. (see Figure 5-32), you can tap the location to open the Maps app and view the location on the screen.

When the event comes up in your calendar, you feel a vibration that alerts you that you have a new notification. Take a look at the screen and you'll see the notification of your upcoming event. Slicker than a box of rocks.

FIGURE 5-32:
The added event title and start and end times appear on the screen.

Chapter 6

Calling Dick Tracy: Voice, Text, and Email

The Gear S2 isn't quite up to Dick Tracy standards of technology yet, but it has come closer than it ever has before. If your Gear S2 connects to your data carrier's network, you can make and receive calls just like the famous (okay, once-upon-a-time famous) detective. You can also make and receive email and text messages through your data carrier's network or through a Wi-Fi connection.

Your Gear S2 isn't connected to a data carrier network, you say? No problem. You can use your smartphone to connect with other people on your Gear S2. Even if you have a data carrier connection, you need to use your smartphone to set up some of the features you need to use voice and message functionality on your smartwatch.

So what smartphones can you use with the Gear S2? If you have a Samsung smartphone running Android 4.4 (KitKat) or a later version, such as Lollipop or Marshmallow, you're good. If you have another brand of Android smartphone, visit the Compatible Android Smartphones page on the Samsung website at http://www.samsung.com/global/galaxy/gear-s2/device-compatibility/. If you have an iPhone, you may want to check the Apple App Store because there was talk about making the iPhone compatible with the Gear S2 as of this writing.

So in this chapter, I start by showing you how to make calls using the Phone app on the Gear S2. You then see how to find contacts to call. Next, I show you how to receive and manage call notifications as well as send and view text and email messages on your Gear S2. Finally, if you want to add more email accounts to check on your smartwatch, you learn how to add an account in the Gear Manager app on your smartphone.

Making and Receiving Calls

I have a Galaxy S6 smartphone that's connected to my Gear S2 Classic with Bluetooth, but you may have purchased your Gear S2 from a phone carrier so that you can make calls on your carrier's data network. In that case, when you send or receive a call, all you have to do is speak into the watch rather than go through your smartphone. (Don't be surprised if you feel the urge to purchase a yellow fedora and trench coat à la Dick Tracy.)

Making a call

To make a call on your Gear S2, follow these steps:

1. **Press the Home button and then tap the Phone icon in the Apps screen (see Figure 6-1).**

   The All Calls screen appears (see Figure 6-2) and displays a log of your calls. If you haven't made any calls, the screen tells you that there are no logs to display.

2. **Tap the Dial Pad icon at the top of the screen.**

   The Dial Pad screen appears with the number icons around the perimeter of the screen. As you tap the icons, the phone number appears in the center of the screen.

   In case you need to dial a phone number with letters in it (such as 1-800-SAMSUNG), you can find letters and other symbols under each number.

FIGURE 6-1:
The Phone app icon is at the 3 o'clock position on the screen.

3. **Tap the Delete icon that appears below the phone number at the center of the screen if you enter a number or symbol by mistake.**

4. **Tap the green Phone icon in the center of the screen (see Figure 6-3) when you've finished entering the number you're calling.**

The phone dial screen appears, and if you have a data carrier connection, the screen tells you that the Gear S2 is making the call.

If you're using your smartphone because you don't have 3G connectivity, the screen tells you that you're making a call on the phone, as you see in Figure 6-4. At this point, you need to pick up your smartphone to start talking.

FIGURE 6-2:
The green dial pad icon appears at the top of the screen.

I can hear that little voice in your head asking why you would place a call on your Gear S2 when you could just use your smartphone to dial. The answer lies in a Bluetooth earpiece. If you have one in your ear, you don't need to use your smartphone to hold a conversation. Instead, it's easier (and cooler) to dial the number on your Gear S2, lower your arm, and use your hands to do something else while you talk.

FIGURE 6-3:
The Phone icon appears above the phone number you dialed.

FIGURE 6-4:
Pick up your smartphone to make the call.

As with a smartphone, when you use your smartwatch you'll carry on a more effective conversation with someone if you speak clearly, hold your watch close enough to your mouth, and speak from a quiet location. You may need to move your arm somewhat toward or away from your head to get the right distance between your mouth and the watch for the person on the other line to hear you clearly.

Receiving a call

When you receive a call on your Gear S2, the smartwatch vibrates, and if you're using a smartphone, it will vibrate as well, depending on your smartphone settings. On your watch, the Incoming Call screen appears, as shown in Figure 6-5, showing who's calling and letting you decide whether to accept or reject the call.

You answer the call by tapping and holding the green answer icon and then swiping to the right. Then hold up the Gear S2 close to your mouth to talk or start talking into your Bluetooth headset if you have one. If you set your Gear S2 to accept voice commands, say "Answer."

FIGURE 6-5:
An incoming call.

If you don't want to take the call, tap and hold the red Reject icon and then swipe to the left. Or just say "Reject" if your Gear S2 accepts voice commands. (Whether you make a face when you say "Reject" is up to you.)

If you don't want to go back to Chapter 3 to learn how to activate the Voice Answer options, here's a quick reminder: Press the Home button and, in the Apps screen, tap the Settings icon. Next, swipe up to Call and then tap it. Now tap Voice Answer. Confirm that you want to use the Voice Answer feature by tapping the Confirm icon on the right side of the screen. You're good to go and can return to the watch screen by pressing the Home button.

Contacting Your Contacts

When you sync your Gear S2 with your smartphone, your Gear S2 also copies everyone in your smartphone's Contacts list so that you don't have to fish for your smartphone in your pocket. Instead, you just access the Contacts list within the Phone app on your Gear S2.

To open your Contacts list, press the Home button on your watch to view the Apps screen. Tap the Phone icon and then, in the screen that appears, tap the Contacts icon (see Figure 6-6).

Browsing your Contacts list

Your Contacts list is divided into categories, starting with the Favorites section. The first contact in the Favorites section is highlighted by default (see Figure 6-7). Swipe up or rotate the bezel to the right to view your name in the My Profile section. Keep swiping up or rotating the bezel to see the entire list of your contents in alphabetical order.

When you find the name of the contact you want to call, tap it. The name appears at the top of the screen and the phone number at the bottom, as shown in Figure 6-8. Call the number by tapping the green Phone icon; you can then talk on either the watch or your smartphone. If you decide you don't need to call this person, press the Back button to return to either the Contacts list or your search.

FIGURE 6-6:
The orange Contacts icon appears at the top of the screen.

FIGURE 6-7:
The first favorite in your list appears in the center of the screen.

Searching for a contact

You can search for a contact by swiping down on the screen or rotating the bezel to the left until the word Search appears in the center of the screen (see Figure 6-9). Tap Search to open the Search screen.

FIGURE 6-8:
The contact photo (if there is one) appears in the background in case you forgot what the contact looks like.

FIGURE 6-9:
After you swipe down, the Search icon appears in the center of the screen.

You may see the Using Keyboard screen if you're using the keyboard for the first time. If you see this, tap the Close icon (it's a blue circle with a white X inside it) at the bottom of the screen. Now you see the keyboard shown in Figure 6-10.

Type the name you want to search for by tapping a given key as many times as necessary to get the required letter to appear. For example, if you want the letter *c*, you tap the number 2 three times in quick succession (about two taps per second). As you tap, you see the letters change until you see the letter *c*.

FIGURE 6-10:
The space key appears below the number 9 in the keypad.

When you're done, stop tapping, and the cursor moves to the next space after the letter *c* so that you can type a new character. Type over the 1 to type a period, comma, question mark, or exclamation point. Type a space by tapping the space key, which appears to the right of the zero key (see Figure 6-10).

You can't use the keypad to enter a number, which is weird because there are numbers on the keypad. Instead, Samsung has decided you should work a little more: You have to rotate the bezel to the right until you see the number keypad. Then you can type in the numbers you want. When you're done, rotate the bezel to the left until you see the alphabetical keypad shown in Figure 6-10.

If your first character is a letter, this letter appears in uppercase by default. After you tap the first letter, all subsequent letters on the keypad are lowercase, which means that the letters you type will be in lowercase unless you use the Shift key. The Shift key is an up arrow and appears to the right of the number 9 in the keypad.

Tap the Shift key once to make the current character uppercase; all the letters in the keypad change to uppercase and the Shift key turns blue. Tap the Shift key again to turn Caps Lock on and type all characters in uppercase. You know when Caps Lock is on because the Shift key changes to a white arrow inside a blue box. Tap the Shift key a third time to turn Caps Lock off and type characters in lowercase.

After you type the first letter, the screen shows you the first entry in the list of contacts that contains that letter anywhere in the contact name (see Figure 6-11). You can type more characters to refine your results. View the entire list of results by tapping the down arrow to the right of the entry in the list.

Swipe up and down the screen (or rotate the bezel left and right) to view the results in the list. When you find the name of the person you want to call, tap the name. In the Call screen that appears (shown in Figure 6-12), tap the Phone icon to call the phone number associated with the contact.

FIGURE 6-11:
The first name that matches your search terms appears in the Search Results screen.

FIGURE 6-12:
The Phone icon is white and is within a transparent white circle.

Finding a Missed Call

If you ever miss a call, the Gear S2 has your back. (Or is it your wrist?) The next time you view the Gear S2 screen, you see the Missed Call screen on your watch. You can call that person back by tapping the name on the screen (see Figure 6-13).

You can return to the watch screen without returning the call by pressing the Home button. At that point, you see a notification reminder in the form of a little orange dot on the left side of the screen, where the 9 o'clock marker is. You can view this notification by swiping from left to right on the screen or by rotating the bezel to the left. Information about the call appears on the Notifications screen.

FIGURE 6-13:
I missed a call from . . . me!

If you decide that you want to use the Phone app to return the call, you'll notice in the Apps screen that the Phone app icon has a little orange dot with a number inside it (see Figure 6-14). That number tells you how many missed calls you have. When you open the Phone app, you can swipe up and down in the Call Log list to see the people who tried to call you.

You can't save voice messages on your watch, but if your Gear S2 is connected to your smartphone with a Bluetooth or Wi-Fi connection, the call also went to your smartphone. If voicemail is set up, you can take out your smartphone and listen to a

FIGURE 6-14:
The orange dot in the Phone app icon shows one missed message.

voicemail message if the caller left one so that you can decide whether to call the person back.

Sending and Reading Text Messages

The Gear S2 is an ideal platform for sending and reading quick text messages. Using your smartwatch's preinstalled Messages app, all you have to do is lift up your wrist, read the message, and type a quick message back if you want (and you'll look cool while you're doing it).

To send a message, follow these steps:

1. **On the watch screen, press the Home button, and in the Apps screen that appears, tap the Messages icon (refer to Figure 6-14).**

   The Messages screen shown in Figure 6-15 appears. If you haven't received any messages, the screen tells you that.

2. **In the text message screen, tap the Send Messages icon at the top of the screen.**

3. **Enter a recipient name in one of two ways:**

   a. *Tap the Enter Recipient icon, shown in Figure 6-16, and then type the name using the keyboard (see "Searching for a contact" for details on using the keyboard, earlier in this chapter).*

   b. *Tap the Contact icon to select from a list of contacts, which is what I do in this example for these steps.*

   The Contacts screen appears and shows you the first contact within the Favorites list, shown in Figure 6-17.

4. **Swipe up and down on the screen (or rotate the bezel left and right) to scroll through all your contact names.**

FIGURE 6-15:
The light orange Send Messages icon appears to the left of the dark orange Contacts icon.

FIGURE 6-16:
The Enter Recipient button appears near the top of the screen.

You can also search for a contact (See "Searching for a contact," earlier in this chapter).

5. **Tap the name in the contact list or the search results list screen when you find the contact who will be the happy recipient of your message.**

If you select a name by accident or decide not to send that person a message, , tap the Delete icon to the right of the name (see Figure 6-18). Otherwise, tap Next at the bottom of the screen.

The first of seven standard text messages that you can send appears on the text message selection screen, shown in Figure 6-19.

6. **Swipe up and down to select the message you want from one of the seven standard text messages if you want.**

When you find one, tap it. If you want to send your own specific text message, jump ahead to "Adding a template message," later in this chapter.

A few seconds after you've selected a standard message or typed one of your own, the Messages app sends the message and displays the Sent screen for a couple of seconds. Then the Messages app home screen reappears and you see the most recent message you sent in the Messages list. The message information includes the message recipient, the message you sent, and the time you sent it (see Figure 6-20).

FIGURE 6-17:
The first favorite in the list appears in the center of the screen.

FIGURE 6-18:
Remove the selected name and start over by tapping the white Delete icon to the right of the name.

You can swipe up and down in the Messages app to view older messages you sent. You can send another message by tapping the New Message icon and going through the preceding steps.

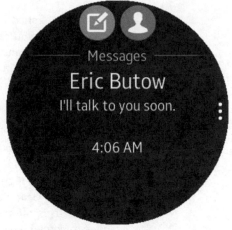

FIGURE 6-19:
The first of seven text messages appears in the center of the screen.

FIGURE 6-20:
The message you just sent appears with other information.

Sending voice, emoji, and short text messages

When you view the screen showing your list of short text messages (refer to Figure 6-19), you see three icons at the top of the screen. These three icons are, from left to right:

>> **The blue voice icon:** Tap to send a voice message.

>> **The purple emoji icon:** Tap to send one or more emojis (also called emoticons) instead of text.

>> **The red keyboard icon:** Tap to type a message with no more than 160 characters.

Swipe down on the screen to enlarge these three icons, as shown in Figure 6-21.

There's a very good reason why you can type only 160 characters in a message: It's the standard limit for Short Message Service (SMS) messages.

FIGURE 6-21:
The three enlarged buttons make tapping them with your finger easier.

SMS was established in 1985 as the standard short message format for mobile devices. Though you can attach photos and videos to SMS messages today, you can't attach photos and videos to SMS messages sent from your Gear S2, so I don't discuss attachments in this book.

Sending a voice message

Tap the blue voice icon to send a voice message. After a second, the Gear S2 vibrates, and you can speak your message (see Figure 6-22). I can attest that the Gear S2 voice recognition system is often quite accurate even when you whisper.

After you stop speaking for a few seconds, the watch displays the text of the message that it thinks you spoke, as shown in Figure 6-23. You can then continue speaking, or tap Tap to Pause at the bottom of the screen. If you've paused, start speaking again by tapping the Speak icon, which is a blue icon with a microphone icon.

If you don't like the text that the Gear S2 translated from your voice, press the Back button to return to the short text messages screen and either try sending another voice message or select another type of message to send.

When you create a voice message, try to be sure to *always* review your message before you press Send. The voice recognition system is good but definitely not perfect, and it can get things spectacularly (and sometimes hilariously) wrong. For example, if you say the word *melancholy* and the screen shows *melon collie,* you probably will want to edit the word . . . unless you like being, um, remarkable.

FIGURE 6-22:
Start speaking when you see Speak Now on the screen.

FIGURE 6-23:
The message appears in the center of the screen — and it's accurate!

If you're happy with the message, send it by tapping the Send icon on the left side of the screen. After a few seconds, the app sends the message and displays the Sent screen for a couple of seconds.

The Messages app returns you to the app's home screen and you see the most recent message that you sent in the Messages list. The message information includes the message recipient, the message you sent, and the time you sent it.

Sending an emoji message

Tap the purple emoji icon to send a message that contains one or more emojis instead of text. In the emoji screen, rotate the bezel left and right to view different emoji in the center of the screen. When you get to the last emoji on the page (a frowning face at about the 11 o'clock position, shown in Figure 6-24), rotate the bezel to the right to see the next page of emojis.

In the second emoji screen page, rotate the bezel to the right to view the rest of the emoji. Rotate the bezel to the left to get back to the crying face at about the 1 o'clock position and then rotate the bezel to the left again to return to the first page of emojis.

FIGURE 6-24:
The selected emoji appears in the center of the screen.

If you don't want to send an emoji, tap the Back icon to return to the short text messages screen. When you find an emoji you want, tap the emoji in the center of the screen to send it.

After a few seconds, the app sends the emoji and displays the Sent screen for a couple of seconds. The Messages app sends you back to the Messages app's home screen and you see the most recent emoji message you sent in the Messages list. The message information includes the message recipient, the emoji you sent, and the time you sent it.

Sending a custom text message

Tap the red keyboard icon to open the custom text message screen and send a text message that you compose yourself. Your message can even include text symbols (explained shortly) and emojis so that your recipient will (or at least should) understand what you're communicating.

In the first page of the custom text message screen, start typing your messages by using the keypad (see the "Searching for a contact" section, earlier in the chapter, for how to use the keypad). As when you type on a smartphone, you can speed finish your message faster by tapping one of the three suggested words that keep appearing as you compose the message (see Figure 6-25). After you type a word, the three suggested words change based on the app thinks you'll want to use next.

The keypad contains a number of pages that allow you to type and add numbers, symbols, and emojis. Rotate the bezel to the right to view and use the numeric keypad, symbol, and emoji keypads. Rotate the bezel to the left to view previous keypads.

The symbols keypad contains a total of five different sub-keypads that are chock-full of symbols for you to use. In the symbols keypad, tap 1/5 to view a sub-keypad with more symbols. The number at the bottom of the screen changes to reflect the sub-keypad of symbols you're on and the total number of sub-keypads. For example, 2/5 means you're on the second sub-keypad of five total sub-keypads. When you reach the last sub-keypad, tap 5/5 to return to the first sub-keypad (1/5).

The emojis keypad also contains three sub-keypads to help you find the right emoji for the emotion you want to represent. In the first emojis sub-keypad, tap 1/3 (the sub-keypad you're on) to move on to view the second sub-keypad of emjois. In the second page, tap 2/3 to go on to the third sub-keypad of emojis. Tapping 3/3 in the third page returns you to the first sub-keypad.

When you're finished with emojis, tap Done at the right side of the keypad. You can view your message in the Compose screen. In the upper-right corner of the compose box, you see the number of characters you've written and the number of total characters you can add (see Figure 6-26).

The number of total characters you have available varies because emojis take up more character space than alphanumeric characters.

You can type more alphanumeric characters by tapping the text in the gray box and then typing on the keypad. If all you mean to send is an emoji, tap the emoji icon in the lower-right corner of the compose box and then select an emoji from the emoji selection screen. If you're in the emoji selection screen and you decide against adding an emoji, just tap the Back icon to return to the Compose screen.

Send the message by tapping the Send icon on the right side of the compose box right above the emoji icon. After a few seconds, the app sends the message and displays the Sent screen for a couple of seconds. The Messages app then displays the app's home screen and shows the most recent message that you sent in the Messages list. The message information includes the message recipient, the message you sent, and the time you sent it.

FIGURE 6-26:
This text message has taken up 10 of 160 available characters.

If you decide that you don't want to send your message, all you have to do is press the Back button. In the Discard Message screen, tap the blue Confirm icon on the right side of the screen, and you go back to the text message selection screen shown previously in Figure 6-19. If you decide you want continue working on your message, tap the Cancel icon at the left side of the Discard Message screen.

Adding a template message

You can also create a custom standard message that Samsung calls a template message. Though it's great that you can create your own template message, here come the caveats: Your message is still limited to 160 characters including spaces, and you have to add this message using the Gear Manager app on your smartphone.

Start the addition process by swiping down on the text message screen and then tapping Add Template (see Figure 6-27).

For a couple of seconds, the screen tells you to add a message on your smartwatch and then returns to the text message selection screen. Turn on your smartphone if it's not on already. The Gear Manager app opens for you automatically and displays the General Messages screen, shown in Figure 6-28. Type the Quick Response message at the top of the screen and then tap the Add icon (the green plus icon) to the right of the Enter Text field.

The new message appears at the top of the short text message list in the General Messages screen (see Figure 6-29). Now turn your eyes back to the Gear S2 screen, and you see that what you added appears in the center of the screen. If the text is longer than what fits on the screen, the text scrolls the first time you see it on the screen.

If your Gear S2 screen turns off before you finish typing your new message, press the Gear S2 Home button to turn on your smartwatch. After you do that, press the Home button again to bring up the Apps screen. Within the Apps screen, tap Recent Apps and then tap the Recent Apps icon. In the Recent Apps screen, you see an image of the Messages app in the center of the screen. Tap the image to open the Messages app and view your new text message on the screen.

FIGURE 6-27:
The Add Template option appears in the center of the screen.

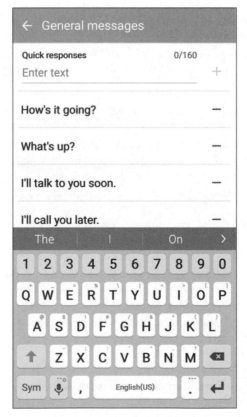

FIGURE 6-28:
As you type, you see what you typed in the Enter Text field.

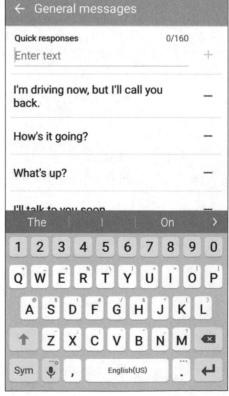

FIGURE 6-29:
The message you added appears at the top of the messages list.

The text message you added will appear every time you open the text message selection screen unless you delete it in Gear Manager. Do this by tapping the Delete icon (it's a red minus icon) to the right of the text message name (refer to Figure 6-28).

Receiving Email in Your Inbox

It's easy to receive email in your inbox because when you set up your Gear S2, your smartwatch was nice enough to synchronize its email accounts with your smartphone email accounts. If you need to add another email account, you can do so in the Gear Manager app. After you add an account, your Gear S2 thinks of you again and syncs with that new account automatically.

Viewing email messages

You can read your email messages on your Gear S2 by following these steps:

1. **Press the Home button to go to the Apps screen.**

2. **Swipe from right to left across the screen (or rotate the bezel to the right) until you see the third and last page on the Apps screen; then tap the Email icon (shown in Figure 6-30).**

   The Email screen, shown in Figure 6-31, display a list of email messages with the subject line and date the message was sent.

3. **Swipe up and down the list to view all the new messages you've received, and open a message by tapping the subject text in the list.**

   If you have no messages, you see the words "No email" on the Email screen.

FIGURE 6-30:
The Email icon appears at the 7 o'clock position on the screen.

Press the Back button to return to the third page of the Apps screen or press the Home button to return to the watch screen.

Adding an email account

If you're not receiving email messages, there's no need to be melancholy because you may not be receiving messages from your desired email account. You can add an email account by following these steps:

1. **Open the Gear Manager app on your smartphone.**

   To start Gear Manager, go to the Home screen, tap the Apps icon, and then swipe right to left as needed to view the page that contains the Gear Manager app. Tap the Gear Manager app icon.

   FIGURE 6-31:
   The most recent message you received appears in the center of the screen.

2. **Tap Settings in the Gear Manager app's home screen.**

3. **Tap Individual App Settings (see Figure 6-32).**

4. **In the Individual App Settings screen, tap Email.**

   The default account you use appears at the top of the Email screen.

5. **Tap Add Account, shown in Figure 6-33.**

6. **In the Email Accounts screen, either select another existing account on your smartphone or type the email address and password in the Enter Sign-In Details. (I do the latter in these steps.)**

   If you enter a Google email account, you see the Google sign-in home page in your smartphone's default web browser, where you enter your Google password. After you enter your Google password, the Enter Account Information screen appears. This screen asks for your permission to have the Email app on your smartphone view and manage your mail and know who you are on Google. Another email service should work similarly.

7. **Tap Allow to return to the Email Accounts window.**

8. **Tap the Set This Account as the Default for Sending Emails check box to set your new account as the default account for sending email messages, or leave it blank and tap Next (see Figure 6-34).**

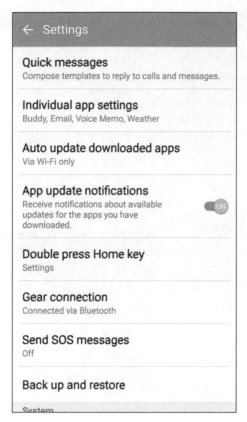

FIGURE 6-32:
The Individual App Settings option is the second option in the list.

FIGURE 6-33:
The Add Account option appears directly underneath the existing account in this example.

9. **In the Sync Settings screen, keep all the default sync settings and then tap Next.**

The Email Accounts window appears again (see in Figure 6-35). You can change the account name and your name for outgoing email messages if you want.

10. **Press Done when you're finished setting up your new email account.**

Now you see the inbox for your added account in the Email app screen within the Gear Manager app. Tap the Back touch button on your smartphone to return to the Email screen. The next time you check for email messages on your Gear S2, new messages will appear from both accounts. Breaking into a celebratory dance is optional.

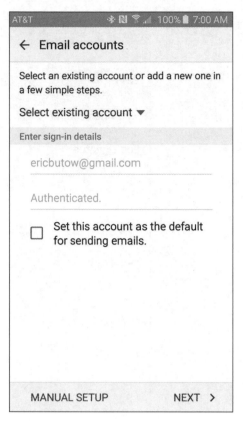

FIGURE 6-34:
Tap Next in the lower-right corner of the screen.

FIGURE 6-35:
The Done option is in red text so that you can find it easily.

Chapter 7

Dancing to the Music: Connecting to Audio

Smartphones are wonderful devices — for the most part. When you use a smartphone to play music, though, it's a pain to keep fishing the phone out of your pocket or unclasping it from a holder to manage your music. Now the Gear S2 frees you from that burden . . . again, for the most part.

Initially, you need to have your smartphone with you to set up the Music Player app on your Gear S2 and get ready to listen to music on the preinstalled Samsung Milk Music app that selects and plays songs for you in a wide variety of categories. After you set up your Gear S2 to play music, however, you can listen smartphone free but there's a catch: You need to purchase a battery-powered Bluetooth headset to listen to your music.

TIP

So where do you find a Bluetooth headset? Typing **Samsung Gear S2 Bluetooth headset** into your favorite web browser will get you started. If you're looking for a Samsung solution so that you can be reasonably sure that the Gear S2 and headset will work together, check out the Samsung Gear Circle headset at http://www.samsung.com/us/explore/gear-circle-features-and-specs/.

In this chapter, I show you how to open the Music Player app on your Gear S2 and play music on your smartphone as well as on a Bluetooth headset. Then you learn how to manage the library in the Music Player app. Next, you find out how to change settings within the Music Player app. You also see how to use the Gear

Manager app on your smartphone to send music to, and store music on, your Gear S2. Finally, this chapter tells you how to use the Samsung Milk Music app to listen to your favorite music in a wide variety of genres.

Playing Your Music

If you're eager to start playing music on your Gear S2, press the Home button to open the Apps screen. Then swipe from right to left on the screen twice or rotate the bezel to the right until you view the third and last page of the Apps screen. Now tap the Music Player icon, shown in Figure 7-1.

The Music Player screen appears with the default song on the screen. If you haven't played a song yet, the song title appears as Unknown.

The Play icon appears in the center of the screen (see in Figure 7-2). Tap the Play Previous icon to the left of the Play Next icon to move to the next song in your phone playlist.

TIP

If you want to skip to another song in your playlist quickly, tap and hold either on the Play Previous icon or the Play Next icon.

You can play music stored on your Gear S2 or stored on your smartphone. By default, you play music on your smartphone through the Bluetooth or Wi-Fi connection between your smartwatch and smartphone. Though your smartphone needs to be on to hear music, you don't need to have the Music app open on your smartphone to play the song.

FIGURE 7-1:
The Music Player icon appears at the 2 o'clock position on the screen.

FIGURE 7-2:
The song title appears below the Play Previous, Play, and Play Next icons.

REMEMBER

When you can't connect your Gear S2 with your smartphone with Bluetooth, be sure that the distance between those two devices is about 32 feet (10 meters) or less. If the two devices are close enough, check the Samsung Gear Support website at http://www.samsung.com/us/support/mobile/galaxy-gear. You can also call Samsung and talk to one of its helpful representatives at 1-800-SAMSUNG (1-800-726-7864).

Start playing the first song in your smartphone's playlist by tapping the Play icon in Figure 7-2. After you start playing the song, the Play icon changes to a Pause icon (two vertical lines), and you can start dancing. Tap the Pause icon to pause the song; tap the Play icon to start playing the song again.

Tap the Volume icon at the top of the screen to adjust the volume level on your smartphone. When you listen to music stored on your Gear S2, tap the Volume icon to change the volume on your smartwatch. The volume level goes from 0, which means silence, to the maximum level of 15. The default volume level is 7.

You can store and play music on your Gear S2. I explain how to store music on your Gear S2 in "Storing Songs on Your Gear S2," later in this chapter. To listen to music stored on your Gear S2, follow these steps:

1. **Tap the Settings icon on the right side of the screen (refer to Figure 7-2).**

    The Settings icon has three vertical dots.

2. **In the Music Player screen that appears, tap the Phone icon (see Figure 7-3) to play music stored on your Gear S2.**

3. **Tap the Confirm icon in the Connect BT Headset screen (see Figure 7-4) to connect your Bluetooth headset to your Gear S2.**

4. **Tap the Confirm icon again to begin the connection process.**

    The Music Player app scans for your Bluetooth headset. If the app can't find the headset, check to make sure that your headset is on and then tap Scan at the bottom of the BT Headset screen to scan for the headset again.

FIGURE 7-3:
The Phone icon appears at the 1 o'clock position on the screen.

If you're still having problems connecting or you would rather get some
other important stuff done such as
managing your music library, press
the Back button to go back to the
Music Player home screen.

Getting around in your music library

On the Music Player screen, shown
in Figure 7-5, an up arrow appears at
the bottom of the screen underneath
a song title and the artist's name. To
get to the Music Player screen, press
the Home button, swipe from right to
left on the screen until you're in the
third page within the Apps screen,
and then tap the Music Player icon
that's at the 2 o'clock position on the
screen.

FIGURE 7-4:
The blue Confirm icon is a white check mark.

Swipe up on the screen to view the
Library screen so that you can take a
gander at your music library. The Gear
S2 includes three songs preinstalled
in your library: "Over the Horizon,"
"Travel," and "Mother Nature."

In the Library screen, the Playing
option is selected by default, as you
can see in Figure 7-6. Swipe up and
down on the screen to view all five of
your Library options, which I cover
shortly. The option you can tap to
select it appears in the center of the

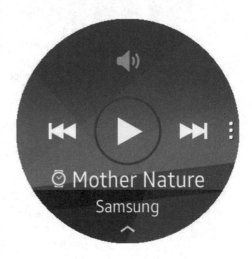

FIGURE 7-5:
The artist's name appears underneath the song title.

screen as you swipe up and down. Within each option screen, you can press the
Back button at any time to return to the Library screen.

The following sections explain the five Library options.

Playing

Tap the Playing option to view the songs in your playlist. The default song, Samsung's "Mother Nature," is already selected. Other songs include "Over the Horizon" and "Travel."

As you swipe up and down the menu to view each song title (see Figure 7-7), the background changes to match the vibe of the song, or at least that is Samsung's intent. Tap the song title to begin playing it in the Music Player home screen.

FIGURE 7-6:
The Playing option appears in the center of the screen by default.

FIGURE 7-7:
Swipe up in the screen to view titles of more songs you can play.

Playlists

Swipe up and down in the Playlists screen (see Figure 7-8) to view one of four playlists:

>> **Favorites:** Contains songs you've marked as favorites, either in the Music app on your smartphone or within the Music Player app on the Gear S2.

>> **Most Played:** The Music Player app keeps track of how many songs you've played and puts these songs in the Most Played playlist so that you can access songs you like more easily.

>> **Recently Played:** Shows you the songs you've played since you last used the Music Player app so that you can listen to one or more of those songs again fast.

>> **Recently Added:** Shows you the songs you've recently added from your smartphone.

If you decide that you're done viewing your playlists but you don't want to play any of the songs, press the Back button to return to the Library screen.

Tracks

Tap Tracks in the Library screen to view a list of all your tracks that are either on your smartphone or your Gear S2, depending on the device you selected in the Play Music From screen. The Tracks screen shown in Figure 7-9 shows you a list of all your tracks so that you can find a specific song to play.

Swipe up and down in the screen (or rotate the bezel to the right and left) to view the entire list. When you see the title of the song you want to play in the center of the screen, tap the song title to start playing it and get your groove on.

Albums

If you're not sure about a title of a song you want to listen to but you know the name of the album that contains the song, tap Albums in the Library screen. The list of albums appears so that you can swipe up and down on the screen to view all albums in the list.

When the album you want is in the center of the screen (see Figure 7-10),

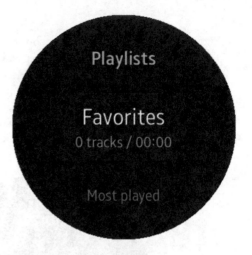

FIGURE 7-8:
Swipe up to view more playlists, such as the songs you've played the most.

FIGURE 7-9:
The track you're playing appears in the center of the screen.

tap the album title to open all tracks contained within the album on the screen. Then you can swipe up and down in the track list screen, and when you see your desired song in the middle of the screen, tap the song title to play it.

Artist

If you're a member of an artist's squad or nation or whatever, you can listen to all songs by one artist by tapping Artist in the Library screen. Next, tap the artist's name in the list that appears (see Figure 7-11).

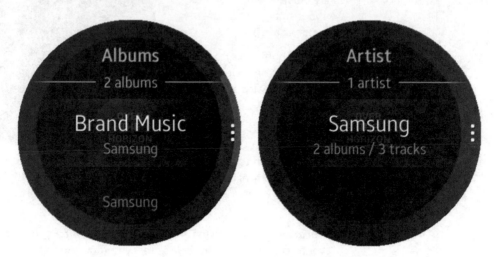

FIGURE 7-10:
Swipe up to view more albums stored on your Gear S2.

FIGURE 7-11:
The number of albums and tracks appear underneath the artist's name in the list.

A list of tracks for the artist appears on the track list screen. Now you can swipe up and down in the screen to view all songs in the list. When your desired song appears in the center of the screen, tap the song title to listen to your song.

Changing settings

When you use the Music Player app on the Gear S2 to play music on your smartphone, you change settings within the Music app on said smartphone. If you play music stored on your Gear S2, you can change settings within the Settings screen.

To change settings in the Music Player app, follow these steps:

1. **Tap the Settings icon on the right side of the screen.**

   The icon looks like three small vertical dots.

2. **Tap Play Music From to open the Play Music From screen.**

3. **Tap the Phone icon.**

4. **Tap any of the following settings icons that appear on the right side of the screen (see Figure 7-12), from top to bottom:**

- **Play Music From:** Play music on your smartphone instead of on your Gear S2.

- **Shuffle:** Shuffles playback of all songs stored on your Gear S2. Tap this icon twice quickly to turn Shuffle off.

- **Repeat:** Tap once to play all songs after you play them. Tap the icon a second time to play the current song again after it's done. Tap the icon a third time to turn the feature off.

FIGURE 7-12:
The Gear icon appears at the 1 o'clock position on the screen.

- **Favorite:** Adds the song to your Favorites playlist. After you tap the Favorite icon, the star turns blue so that you know the song is a favorite. You can remove the song as a favorite by tapping the Favorite icon again, which makes the star turn white with a blue outline.

Storing Songs on Your Gear S2

Another way the Music Player app on your Gear S2 is tethered to your smartphone is that you need to download music to your smartphone and then send that music to your Gear S2 within the Gear Manager app on your smartphone.

Fortunately, Samsung makes the downloading process pretty easy. (No, really.) Start by opening the Gear Manager app on your smartphone and then tapping Send Content to Gear, as shown in Figure 7-13.

REMEMBER

To open Gear Manager, tap the Apps icon on the Home screen, swipe from right to left in the Apps screen if necessary to view the page with the Gear Manager icon, and then tap the Gear Manager icon.

With the Send Content to Gear screen open, follow these steps to send music to your Gear S2:

1. **Tap Select Tracks (see Figure 7-14), which is under the orange menu bar at the top of the screen.**

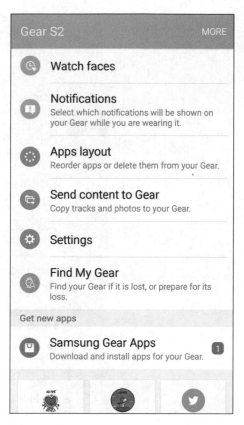

FIGURE 7-13:
The Send Content to Gear option is the fourth option in the list.

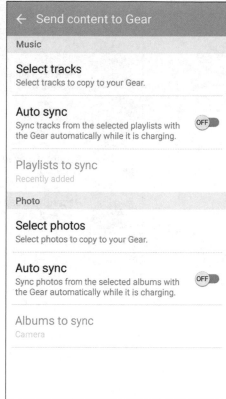

FIGURE 7-14:
The Select Tracks option.

A list of playlists appears as shown in Figure 7-15. This list mirrors the list of playlists you saw in the Music Player app on your Gear S2. That is, the list includes Favorite Tracks, Most Played, Recently Played, and Recently Added.

2. **Tap the playlist you want to add, which in this example is Recently Added.**

3. **In the screen of the playlist you chose, tap the check box to the left of the track you want to add.**

   The check box turns green and contains a white check mark. Repeat this process by tapping all check boxes for tracks you want to add. You may need to swipe up and down in the screen to view all the tracks.

   If you want to select all tracks, save yourself some time by tapping the All check box at the top of the page (see Figure 7-16).

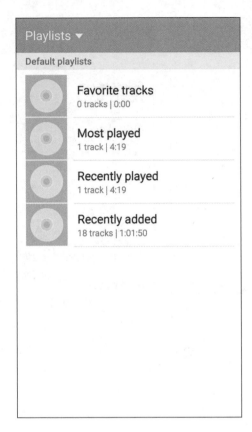

FIGURE 7-15:
Each playlist entry includes the number of tracks and the length of all the tracks combined.

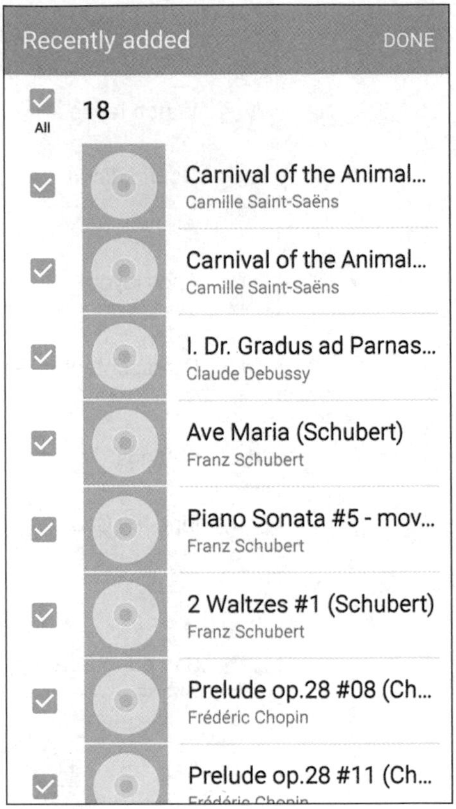

FIGURE 7-16:
Tap the All check box to select all tracks automatically.

4. **Tap Done (at the right side of the orange menu bar at the top of the screen) when you're finished.**

   A pop-up box appears at the bottom of the screen with the word Sending. Depending on the number of songs you added, you may need to wait a few minutes for the smartphone to send all the tracks to your Gear S2.

   When the copying process is done, you see a pop-up box informing you of this feat at the bottom of your smartphone screen.

To confirm that the song you intended to load onto your Gear S2 really did make it (and to play it, if you want), follow these steps:

1. **Open the Music Player app on the watch and swipe up on the app's home screen.**

2. **Tap and hold on the up arrow at the bottom of the screen and then swipe up to open the Library screen.**

3. **Swipe up on the screen until Playlists appears in the center (see Figure 7-17).**

4. **Tap Playlists.**

5. **In the Playlists screen, swipe up.**

6. **When you see Recently Added in the center of the screen (see Figure 7-18), tap it.**

FIGURE 7-17:
When you see the Playlists option in the center of the screen, tap Playlists.

FIGURE 7-18:
The number of tracks and the length of all the tracks combined appears under the Recently Added playlist name.

7. **Swipe up and down to view the list of songs you can play in your playlist.**

The song in the center of the screen has larger white text to denote that it's selected. The artist name appears underneath, as shown in Figure 7-19. If no artist is associated with the song name, you see Unknown.

If the selected song title is too long to fit on the screen, you see the title scroll once so that you can see the entire title. When the title finishes scrolling, you see just the beginning of the title (enough to fit on the screen).

FIGURE 7-19:
The artist name appears underneath the song title.

8. **Tap the title in the list to start listening to the track.**

If you have to connect a Bluetooth headset, turn on the headset and then tap the Confirm icon within the Connect BT Headset screen (refer to Figure 7-4).

Listening to Your Internet Radio

The Gear S2 comes preinstalled with Samsung's Milk Music app. (I'm as baffled as you are about how Samsung came up with this name.) You use this app with the Samsung Milk Music app on your smartphone to listen to songs in a variety of categories. These songs are suggested by Samsung, and as you add songs to your list of favorites, you create your own customized radio station with all your favorite songs. What's more, you can listen to a variety of sports talk radio stations from around the United States with Milk Music.

Before you can use the Milk Music app, you need to set it up on both your Gear S2 and your smartphone. To do so, follow these steps:

1. **On your Gear S2, press the Home button to open the Apps screen and then swipe from right to left twice to open the third page in the Apps screen (or rotate the bezel to the right until you view the third page).**

2. **Tap Samsung Milk Music (see Figure 7-20).**

   The Samsung Milk Music app screen opens.

3. **Tap OK (see Figure 7-21) to open the Galaxy Apps app on your smartphone and view the Details screen for the Companion for Samsung Milk Music Gear S2 app.**

4. **On your smartphone, tap the blue Install icon, shown in Figure 7-22, to install the Milk Music Gear S2 app.**

   The Permissions window appears. You can provide access to your smartphone resources by tapping Accept and Download.

FIGURE 7-20:
The Samsung Milk Music icon appears at the 3 o'clock position on the screen.

After your smartphone installs the Milk Music Gear S2 app, move your eyes to the Gear S2. If the Gear S2 screen is off, you'll have to return to the Apps screen on your smartwatch. You can do this either by pressing the Home button or by moving your arm up closer to your head so that you can see the screen. Then you can press the Home button to open the Apps screen.

5. **On the third page in the Apps screen, tap the Milk Music icon.**

6. **In the Apps screen that appears, tap the Milk Music icon.**

   The Milk Music app starts and asks you to add the Milk Music widget for quick access. This message is there to remind you to add the widget when you finish installing the Milk Music app. You can learn about adding the Milk Music widget by bookmarking this page and then read Chapter 5 to learn about the wonderful world of widgets.

7. **Tap OK (see Figure 7-23) to continue with the Milk Music app setup process.**

   If this is your first time using Milk Music, you need to sign into Milk Music on your smartphone, as described in the following step.

8. **When you see the Milk Music terms and conditions screen on your smartphone, tap I Agree.**

9. **In the Milk Music app on your Gear S2, tap the check mark icon at the top of the screen and when the Apps screen appears, tap the Milk Music icon.**

   Now you see the Milk Music home screen and can listen to your favorite music or talk radio source, which I tell you more about in the next section.

FIGURE 7-21:
Tap OK at the bottom of the screen.

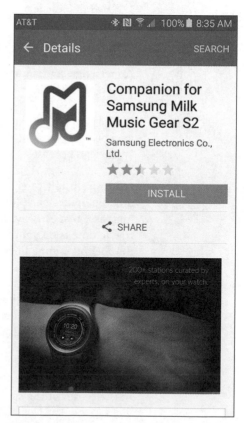

FIGURE 7-22:
The blue Install icon appears underneath the app title, app developer name, and the aggregated review score.

Getting comfortable with Milk Music

After you have the Milk Music app set up on both your phone and Gear S2, the featured song of the day appears on the Gear S2 screen with the title of the song and the name of the artist, as well as a photo of the artist in the background. You can play the song on your smartphone, and learn what your reaction is to modern music, by tapping the Play icon at the bottom of the Gear S2 screen.

FIGURE 7-23:
Tap OK at the bottom of the screen to close it.

When you play the song on your Gear S2, the Milk Music app opens on your smartphone as well. You can turn off the smartphone screen if you don't want to view it, but you'll still hear the music from your smartphone's speakers.

REMEMBER

Some songs contain a prerecorded introduction and some other commercial stuff from a Milk Music host. It's the price you pay for a free service.

On the Gear S2, you can pause playback in the Milk Music app by tapping the Pause icon at the bottom of the screen (see Figure 7-24). While the song is paused, the Pause icon becomes a Play icon. You tap the Play icon to resume playing the song.

Swipe from left to right on the Milk Music screen to change the playback volume on your smartphone. Then rotate your bezel left and right to decrease and increase, respectively, the smartphone volume. You'll be able to hear how loud the volume is on your smartphone and see the corresponding volume level in the number of volume lines that light up around the perimeter of the Gear S2 screen (see Figure 7-25).

After you stop changing the volume, the Milk Music home screen reappears on your Gear S2 after a few seconds. Now swipe the screen from right to left to open the Song Selection page and see how many more featured songs are available to you.

The number of songs available in this category appears within the Play Next icon in the center of the screen (for example, Figure 7-26 shows the number 6). After you tap the Play Next icon, the next featured song starts playing in the Milk Music app on your smartphone. The Milk Music app's home screen appears on the Gear S2 so that you can see the song title and artist name.

FIGURE 7-24:
Tap the Pause icon to pause playback.

FIGURE 7-25:
As you turn up the volume, more volume lines light up.

When you're looking at the Milk Music home screen, swipe the screen from right to left twice to view the Favorites screen. Tap the Favorite icon shown in Figure 7-27 to save the song in your Favorite Songs playlist; when you do so, the heart icon turns white.

FIGURE 7-26:
The number of songs appears within the triangle portion of the Play Next icon.

FIGURE 7-27:
The Favorite icon is a heart that appears in the center of the screen.

Finding your listening taste

When you're in the Milk Music app's home screen, you use the bezel to select from the seemingly endless list of music categories, online sports, and other types of radio stations you can choose from.

As you move down the list, you can move back up the list by rotating the bezel to the left. The selected category is highlighted on the screen shown in Figure 7-28.

When you find a category you like, tap it. The first of six songs in that category starts playing. You can open the Song Selection page and play another song by swiping from right to left and tapping the Play Next icon.

FIGURE 7-28:
The highlighted category appears in the center of the screen.

TIP

When you tap the Play Next icon, it's possible that you'll hear more than one commercial before you hear the next song. The Milk Music app is free because it's supported by commercials, so you have to suffer and listen to these commercials in their entirety before Milk Music plays the next song. You may have already thought of the solution of turning the volume down or even mute the speaker while the commercial plays, but you probably thought of the downside, too: You might miss hearing the beginning of the next song.

Press the Back button to return to the Apps screen, press the Home button to return to the watch screen.

Streaming audio without your smartphone

You don't need to have your smartphone on the next time you start Milk Music on your Gear S2. After you start Milk Music on your smartwatch while your smartphone is off, you see the Now in Standalone Mode screen. Tap the check mark at the top of the screen to continue (see Figure 7-29). (But first, if you don't want to show this screen the next time you enter Standalone Mode, tap the Do Not Show check box.) Then follow these steps to go solo (via a Wi-Fi connection) on your Gear S2:

1. **Tap the Confirm icon on the right side of the Connect via Wi-Fi screen that you see in Figure 7-30 to connect to Milk Music using your Wi-Fi connection.**

TIP

(If it's not a good time to connect after all, tap the Cancel button on the left side of the screen. Confirm your cancellation by tapping the Cancel icon on the left side of the screen, and you return to the Apps screen.)

After you tap the Confirm icon in the Connect via Wi-Fi screen, the Wi-Fi settings screen appears. If you're not connected to a Wi-Fi network, you see Not Connected underneath the Wi-Fi Networks option.

2. **Swipe up and tap Wi-Fi Networks (see Figure 7-31).**

3. **Swipe up and down in the Wi-Fi networks list, and when you see the network you want to connect to in the center of the screen, tap the network name.**

You may need to enter a password (see Chapter 3 for details about entering a password).

4. **Press the Home button to return to the watch screen.**

5. **Press the Home button in the watch screen to open the Apps screen.**

You see the apps page with the Samsung Milk Music icon.

6. **Tap the Milk Music icon to open Milk Music again.**

7. **In the Now in Standalone Mode screen, tap the check mark icon at the top of the screen to continue.**

FIGURE 7-29:
The Now in Standalone Mode screen.

FIGURE 7-30:
The blue Confirm icon has a white check mark inside it.

You have to connect a Bluetooth headset to listen to your music, so the Please Connect a Bluetooth Headset screen asks you to confirm that your headset is ready to connect.

8. **Make sure that your headset is on and then tap the Confirm icon on the right side of the screen to continue (see Figure 7-32).**

The BT Headset screen appears and scans for your Bluetooth headset. When the Gear S2 finds the headset, you can listen to your songs on Milk Music right from your Gear S2. And because your sturdy Gear S2 will stay strapped to your wrist, go ahead and dance like no one's watching.

FIGURE 7-31:
Tap Wi-Fi Networks to connect.

FIGURE 7-32:
The Confirm icon sports a white check mark.

Chapter 8

Getting Help from S Voice

Your Gear S2 functionality goes farther than the creators of the Dick Tracy comic strip ever imagined. Not only can you download apps to run on your Gear S2 (as detailed in Chapter 10), but the intrepid detective would be jealous at your ability to speak commands to your Gear S2 using the built-in S Voice app.

In this chapter, you learn how to set up and use S Voice so you that can speak commands to your Gear S2 and give your fingers a break. The chapter starts by showing you how to start S Voice and speak commands to get information such as where your nearest restaurants are. Next, you find out how to wake up your Gear S2 using your voice. You also see how to tell S Voice what language you're speaking and how to reset S Voice and restore the app's default settings.

Starting Up S Voice

Before you start using S Voice, you should make sure that your microphone isn't obstructed so that your Gear S2 can hear your voice clearly. Where is your microphone, you ask? Just look for the small dot in between the Back and Home buttons on the right side of the watch. (That is, it's the right side when you're looking at the watch face.)

TIP

Make sure that your finger isn't on the microphone when you start talking into your watch. This is more likely to happen if you don't have the watch strapped to your wrist and you're not pressing either button on the watch.

Not blocking your microphone is probably the most obvious thing you can do to ensure that your Gear S2 can hear you, but here are some other tips to help the S Voice app understand you:

>> **Speak clearly.** That is, enunciate your words and don't have food in your mouth.

>> **Speak in quiet places.** If you're trying to speak to your Gear S2 on a busy city street or at a rock concert, chances are your watch won't understand you at all.

>> **Don't use obscenities or slang words.** If you find that S Voice isn't understanding what you're saying, try speaking another word for the same term.

>> **Avoid speaking in dialectal accents.** If you speak your language with an accent, S Voice may either not understand you or may think that you're speaking a different word than what you intend. If S Voice has trouble with your speaking style, talking to your Gear S2 may not be an option for you.

To get started with S Voice, follow these steps:

1. **Press the Home button and then tap the S Voice icon (see Figure 8-1).**

   The Set Command screen appears first so that you can set your own wake-up command for the Gear S2.

2. **Tap the Cancel icon on the left side of the screen, shown in Figure 8-2.**

   This closes the Set Command screen and opens the app's home screen. (Later in this chapter, when you access S Voice settings, you see how to wake up the Gear S2 using S Voice.)

FIGURE 8-1:
The S Voice icon is at about the 9 o'clock position on the screen.

The S Voice home screen gives you a couple of suggestions for speaking commands. At the bottom of the screen, you see a blue area that displays the audio signal waveform. When you speak, the waveform changes, indicating that the Gear S2 has picked up your voice in the microphone.

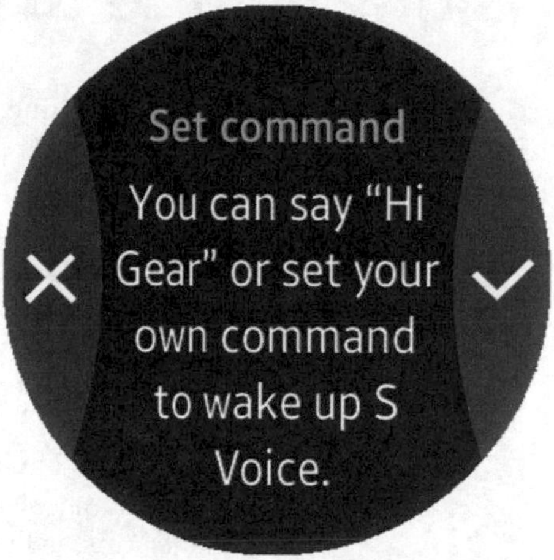

3. **Tap the Help icon at the top of the screen (see Figure 8-3) to get more suggestions of commands to give S Voice.**

4. **Swipe up and down the screen to view more suggested ways you can speak to your Gear S2, such as how to dial a phone number by saying the word "dial" followed by the phone number.**

FIGURE 8-2:
The Cancel icon contains a white *X*.

5. **Tap the blue microphone icon at the bottom of the screen (see Figure 8-4) and speak a command.**

FIGURE 8-3:
The Help icon is a white circle with a question mark inside it.

FIGURE 8-4:
The blue microphone icon includes an icon of . . . a microphone!

Asking S Voice to Find Something

After you stop talking, S Voice takes a few seconds to think about what you said and shows the words on the screen. Your Gear S2 is very good at translating your voice to text, and my own personal experiences proved that the Gear S2 can hear whispers well, too.

However, if S Voice couldn't understand you for some reason, a polite message appears on screen (see Figure 8-5) informing you of that fact. Speak your message again to give S Voice another chance. You may want to hold the watch a little closer to your head to see whether that helps. If it doesn't, remember to speak clearly in a quiet environment and avoid slang; also try to minimize any accent you have. You may also want to try a different term for your search, such as "find restaurants" instead of the actual restaurant name.

For this example, I spoke the command "Find Togo's" so that I could find the location of the restaurant near me that serves yummy sandwiches. S Voice understood my request and showed a list of restaurants near me, including Togo's. When you see a list of restaurants, swipe up and down in the results screen (see Figure 8-6) until you see the restaurant you're looking for in the center of the screen.

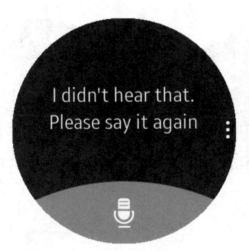

FIGURE 8-5:
S Voice tells you politely that it didn't hear what you said.

FIGURE 8-6:
S Voice uses your Gear S2 GPS functionality to tell you how far each restaurant is from your current location.

Tap an establishment's name to view more information about it, including the address (see Figure 8-7).

It seems a bit odd to this humble author that you can't tap on the address on the screen to open the Maps app and find the location on your watch screen. Although we may see that in a future version of S Voice, for now you need to use your smartphone to look for the location on a map. But you can also use your Gear S2 (or your smartphone) to call the restaurant to get more information. On your Gear S2, just swipe up in the screen shown previously in Figure 8-7 and then tap Call.

FIGURE 8-7:
Information about the place you've searched for, including the distance from your current location, appears onscreen.

Changing S Voice Settings

Before you start using S Voice in your everyday life, you may want to review the S Voice settings and change the ones that will help you use S Voice the way you want. To get to your S Voice settings, go to the S Voice home screen and tap the Settings icon on the right side of the screen. The icon looks like three small vertical dots.

TIP

Actually, the Settings icon is also available in many other S Voice screens, including the results screen so you don't necessarily have to return to the home screen to access the Settings screen.

Turning Voice Wake-Up on and off

You can instruct your Gear S2 to come out of its sleep just by using your voice. To do so, tap the Settings icon, and you see four icons at the right side of the Settings screen, as shown in Figure 8-8. The Voice Wake-Up icon is selected by default, which means the Wake-Up feature is active so that you can set the wake-up command, as you learn to do in the upcoming section, "Teaching your watch to wake up."

If you prefer to use your finger to press the Home button to wake up your Gear S2, or if talking to your smartwatch will bring you some curious or even dirty looks, you can turn off the Wake-Up feature by tapping the Voice Wake-Up icon.

When the Wake-Up feature is off, all you have to do to turn it on again is tap the Voice Wake-Up icon. The Voice Wake-Up screen appears, and you just tap the Confirm icon on the right side of the screen to turn it on.

FIGURE 8-8:
The Voice Wake-Up icon appears at the 1 o'clock position on the screen and has a blue icon, which means the setting is on.

REMEMBER

You don't need to use your voice to wake up your Gear S2 every time. You can still press the Home button or just lift up your wrist so that your smartwatch understands that it's time to wake up.

Teaching your watch to wake up

After you know that Voice Wake-Up is on, you can train your Gear S2 to understand your spoken command to turn your smartwatch screen on. Put S Voice in class by tapping the Set Wake-Up Command icon on the screen, as shown in Figure 8-9.

S Voice requires you to say your wake-up command four times to ensure that it understands what you're saying when you want the Gear S2 to wake up. So be sure to keep your command short and to the point, and it may be a good idea to include the word "Gear" in the wake-up command so that people around you don't think you're telling them to wake up.

FIGURE 8-9:
The Set Wake-Up Command icon is at the 2 o'clock position on the screen.

To train S Voice to understand your wake-up command, follow these steps:

1. **In the Set Command screen, tap Start shown in Figure 8-10.**

2. **Say the wake-up command.**

   You could say something simple, like "Wake up." When you stop talking, S Voice takes a second or two to understand what you said. Then S Voice moves to the second step in the training process. Under the "Speak Now" text on the screen, you see "(1/4)." This means that you completed the first step of the four-step training process. Completing the second step shows "(2/4)" (see Figure 8-11), and so on.

3. **Repeat the rotation and speaking steps three more times, and say the wake-up command (the same one you spoke in Step 2) each time.**

   After you say your wake-up command the fourth time, S Voice will analyze your commands and make sure that it understands all four commands. If the Gear S2 didn't hear you properly during one or more of the steps, you see the Fail screen, shown in Figure 8-12. In that case, tap the Confirm icon at the right side of the screen to record the four wake-up commands again.

   After S Voice successfully recognizes your wake-up command, you see the Success screen that tells you that you're successful.

4. **Tap the OK icon at the bottom of the screen to return to the S Voice home screen.**

FIGURE 8-10:
Tap Start at the bottom of the screen.

FIGURE 8-11:
The second step in the four-step training process.

REMEMBER

If you don't have the Voice Wake-Up feature on, talking to your Gear S2 to wake it up won't work, obviously. So don't get frustrated and start yelling at your watch! Instead, press the Home button, open the S Voice app, and turn the Voice Wake-Up feature back on. If the Voice Wake-Up feature is on but your voice isn't waking up the watch, try recording a new wake-up command. And if that doesn't work, call Samsung (1-800-SAMSUNG) so that a Samsung customer representative can help you figure out what's ailing your Gear S2.

FIGURE 8-12: You need to tap the Confirm icon to train S Voice further.

TIP

If you want to change your wake-up command after you've recorded one, all you have to do is go back to the Settings screen and tap the Set Wake-Up Command icon again. After you tap the icon, the Change Command screen appears and asks whether you really want to change your wake-up command. Tap the Confirm icon on the right side of the screen to record a new command, or tap the Cancel icon on the left side of the screen to keep your current wake-up command.

Changing your language in S Voice

Instead of watching your language, you can change your language on your smartwatch. Now that you've stopped groaning, it's important to remember that although the default language on the Gear S2 is English, S Voice can understand several languages, so you may be able to use your native language to make the Gear S2 do your bidding.

To change the language your S Voice responds to, follow these steps:

1. **In S Voice, tap the icon that displays as three small vertical dots to open the Settings screen.**

2. **Tap the Language icon (see Figure 8-13).**

   The Language screen appears, as shown in Figure 8-14.

FIGURE 8-13:
The Language icon appears at the 3 o'clock position on the screen.

FIGURE 8-14:
The Automatic option is selected by default, which is English (United States).

3. **You can swipe up and down in the screen (or rotate the bezel to the right and left) to view the following list of languages to choose from:**

   - *English (United States)*

   - *Español (América Latina)*

   - *Français (France)*

   - *Chinese*

   - *Korean*

4. **Tap a language to select it.**

   You see all the text within the S Voice app on the screen in your selected language. The next time you open the Language screen, you see your current language in the center of the screen. At that point, you can swipe up and down in the screen to select a new language.

REMEMBER

This language change applies only to the S Voice app. When you exit S Voice, you see text on the screen that applies to the rest of the Gear S2. If you want to change the language for the Gear S2 as well, check out Chapter 3 to learn how to change the language in the Settings app.

Resetting S Voice

If you want to return S Voice to its default options for whatever reason, open the Settings screen and then tap the Reset S Voice icon (see Figure 8-15).

Swipe up and down in the screen to view the entire message that serves as both information and a warning about what will happen when you reset S Voice. Begin the reset process by tapping the Confirm icon on the right side of the screen (see Figure 8-16).

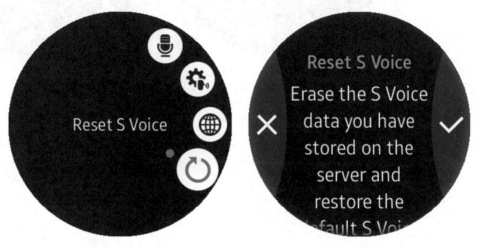

FIGURE 8-15:
The Reset S Voice icon appears at the 4 o'clock position on the screen.

FIGURE 8-16:
The Confirm icon is a white check mark.

After you reset S Voice, you return to the Apps screen. Tap the S Voice icon to open the S Voice app again. You're greeted by the Set Command screen, which invites you to set your wake-up command as described earlier in this chapter.

To keep all your current settings after all, tap the Cancel icon on the left side of the screen. Now you can start talking to your watch, and if you encounter people who wonder what you're doing, you can take the opportunity to tell people about your Gear S2 and how it has improved your life since you strapped it on your wrist.

Chapter 9

Shaping Up with S Health

Samsung designed the Gear S2 with helping you to monitor your physical health in mind. Samsung includes a pair of heart rate sensors that light up when the watch scans your wrist for your heart rate, plus your Gear S2 comes installed with the S Health app, which you can use to track your activities and inspire you to stay true to your exercise goals and fluid intake.

S Health can tell you how you exercise over a typical day to help you determine whether you need to change how you behave to get more exercise. After you change your behavior, you can monitor your activity over a 24-hour period again and take note of the changes. The end result could be a happier you who gets straight, goes forward, and moves ahead.

In this chapter, you start by learning how to access the S Health app and how the app tracks your activity throughout a 24-hour day. Then you find out how to monitor your daily steps, your exercise regimen, your heart rate, and your fluid intake. Finally, you see how to change S Health settings so that the app can provide fitness recommendations based on your age, gender, and other factors.

REMEMBER

The information provided by S Health isn't designed to diagnose any problems with your health. However, it will give you important data that you can use to change how you treat your body and perhaps see your doctor when you see something curious like a high heart rate while you're resting.

Tracking Your Active Day

The S Health app is easy to find within the Apps screen. Just press the Home but-ton and then tap the S Health icon in the Apps screen, as shown in Figure 9-1.

The first thing the S Health app does is check to see whether your smartwatch is on your wrist. If you don't have your smartwatch on, you get a big reminder that you need to wear your Gear S2, as you see in Figure 9-2.

FIGURE 9-1:
The S Health icon appears at the 4 o'clock posi-tion on the Apps screen.

FIGURE 9-2:
Put your Gear S2 on your wrist to start tracking.

After you put your Gear S2 on, or if you have it on your wrist already, you see the tracking screen. A black ring appears around the perimeter of the screen, and this ring contains tick marks evenly spaced around the ring. Each tick mark represents 30 minutes, and there are numbers for 6 hours, 12 hours, 18 hours, and 24 hours of activity at the right, bottom, left, and top sides of the screen, respectively.

When you view the S Health tracking screen, you see a line next to the black ring that represents the type of activity you've had over the course of the day. White represents inactivity, yellow indicates light activity, and green represents health-ful activity such as active exercise.

The S Health app starts tracking specific activities only when you tell it to start. You can start tracking your activity by tapping Start (see Figure 9-3).

After you start tracking, an orange dot shows you where you are in the 24-hour monitoring process. In the example shown in Figure 9-4, the dot appears at about 12 hours and 30 minutes into the 24-hour monitoring period. Even when I'm sitting down and typing on my computer writing this book, the status in the middle of the screen shows me that I'm doing light activity.

FIGURE 9-3:
Tap Start at the bottom of the screen.

FIGURE 9-4:
Your Gear S2 bucks you up by telling you that your activity level is not bad.

If you want to know more than the fact that you're doing a good job with your exercise, tap the exercise status, such as Not Bad (refer to Figure 9-4). The current number of steps you've taken with healthful, light, and little-to-no activity appears on the screen.

REMEMBER

If you're sitting around for more than an hour, S Health considers you inactive and gives you an alert to get up and walk around so that you don't turn into a lifeless sack of protoplasm. S Health likes it best if you're walking 100 steps per minute for at least 10 minutes straight.

Monitoring Your Body

The S Health app goes beyond just tracking your activity over a 24-hour period. It also helps you track your exercise and the fluids you take in.

Tracking your steps

To track your steps, start from the S Health tracking screen and rotate the bezel to the right until you feel the bezel click. You should be in the Track Your Steps screen.

This screen shows the number of steps you've taken (see Figure 9-5) and see how that number compares to the daily steps goal you've set. (You learn how to change the goal later in this chapter.)

FIGURE 9-5:
The default goal for the number of steps you should take each day is 6,000.

Recording your exercise

From the Track Your Steps screen (the previous section tells you how to get to this screen), rotate the bezel to the right until you feel the bezel click. Now you see the Exercise screen, which asks you to tap the Start icon to start recording the exercise you want (see in Figure 9-6).

REMEMBER

After you tap Start, you may see the Set Up Profile screen asking you to set up your profile. You can set up your profile by tapping the green Confirm icon on the right side of the screen and then making your profile changes in the Profile screen. I show you how to set up your profile in the "Changing S Health Settings" section, later in this chapter. For now, proceed to the exercise type screen by tapping the Cancel icon on the left side of the Set Up Profile screen.

FIGURE 9-6:
The Start icon is a right-pointing arrow.

When the exercise type screen appears (see Figure 9-7), you can choose from one of the following eight types, which are represented as icons around the perimeter of the screen, from right to left:

» Running

» Walking

» Cycling

» Hiking

» Elliptical trainer

» Exercise bike

» Step machine

» Treadmill

FIGURE 9-7:
The eight icons represent the eight types of exercise you can record.

What you can do next to set up the goals for your exercise type depends on that exercise type. I tap the Walking icon because I like to walk around my hilly, rural neighborhood to get some good exercise. (If the local gang of turkeys has decided to walk on the road at the same time, running away is also good exercise.)

One neat feature of S Health is the capability to check your location when you're exercising outdoors. That is, when you're tracking the Running, Walking, Cycling, or Hiking exercise types, you see the Use Location-Based Features screen. When you have Location-Based Features on, you also see a map of where you traveled after you stop monitoring and can view a summary of your walk.

For this feature to work, you need to have both your Gear S2 and smartphone on, with the Location service on your smartphone turned on. If you meet that criteria, turn on Location-Based Features by tapping the Confirm icon on the right side of the screen. If you don't, tap the Cancel icon on the left of the screen.

After you turn Location-Based Features on or off, you see the Set Target screen, which lets you set a desired target. For the Walking exercise type, you can swipe your finger from right to left on the screen (or rotate the bezel to the right) to choose from one of four target types:

» **The time target:** The default time is 30 minutes, but you can change the time by tapping the screen, rotating the bezel right and left until you see the desired time on the screen, and then tapping Set.

» **The target distance:** This distance is two miles by default. You change the distance by tapping the target, rotating the bezel right and left until you see your desired distance on the screen, and then tapping Set.

>> **The target calories burned:** This target is 300 calories by default. As with the time and distance targets, you change the calorie target by tapping the screen, rotating the bezel left and right until you see the desired calorie count on the screen, and then tapping Set.

>> **A basic workout:** This target type has no specific target. For example, you may want to walk to a specific location and back, which doesn't need you to set a target to know that you met your goal.

When you've select a target type or finished modifying your selected target type, tap Start (see Figure 9-8).

The screen gives you a three-second countdown before it starts to monitor your walk. You see the elapsed time in the Duration screen. Rotate the bezel to the right to view various monitoring screens (see Figure 9-9) that include the following:

>> **Distance:** The distance you've traveled so far

>> **Calories:** The number of calories you've burned so far

>> **Speed:** Your current speed

>> **Heart Rate:** Your current heart rate

FIGURE 9-8:
Tap Start at the bottom of the screen.

FIGURE 9-9:
Your heart rate appears at a resting rate until you start your exercise.

Note that at the bottom of the Duration, Distance, Calories, and Speed screens, you see your current heart rate. At the bottom of the Heart Rate screen, you see the elapsed time.

While you're viewing the monitoring screen, tap the screen to pause or finish tracking before you reach your goal. You can also listen to music stored on your Gear S2 or within the Samsung Milk Music app on your smartphone by rotating the bezel to the left until you see the Open Music screen.

Tap the Music icon in the center of the screen (it looks like a musical note) to open the Music Player app. Tap the Play icon to start listening to the first song that the Milk Music app chose for you within your selected music category on your smartphone. Tap the Pause icon, which replaces the Play icon while you're playing the song, to stop playing the song. If you want to learn how to change the songs you listen to in Milk Music, as well as change the settings in the Music Player app, Chapter 7 tells you all about it.

If you want to monitor your exercise progress while still listening to music, press the Back button. The Open Music screen appears, and you can rotate the bezel to the right to view the monitoring screens.

TIP

After you close the S Health app, the Music Player app is still on. You can close this app from the watch face screen by pressing the Home button and then tapping the Recent Apps icon at the 1 o'clock position within the Apps screen. If you have more than one app open, you may need to swipe from right to left until you see the Music Player screen image in the center of the screen. Close the Music Player app by tapping the Delete icon (it looks like a red *X* inside a white circle) in the upper-right corner of the Music Player screen image.

After you finish tracking your exercise, you see the summary screen that shows you how much of your goal was achieved, how long you walked, the distance you walked, and how many calories you burned on the walk. You can also swipe your finger up and down (or rotate the bezel right and left) to view more detailed information, including your average walking speed and a map of where you walked.

When you're done reviewing your walk information, press the Back button to return to the Summary List screen, shown in Figure 9-10, and view a list of your walk summaries. The most recent summary appears at the top of the list.

Return to the Exercise screen by pressing the Back button. The Exercise screen shows you how long you walked during your last exercise.

When you finish tracking your exercise, S Health saves your monitoring information on the Gear S2 in log files. If you have your smartphone on and S Health is installed on your smartphone, the Gear S2 saves that monitoring data to your smartphone as well. S Health on your Gear S2 doesn't save many log files, so if you don't see your log file, the S Health app on your smartphone likely has that log file saved. S Health doesn't save any data if you have monitored yourself for fewer than two minutes.

Measuring your heart rate

To find out your heart rate after you've been exercising, from the Exercise screen, rotate the bezel to the right until you feel the bezel click. You should be in the Heart Rate screen (see Figure 9-11), and you can measure your heart rate by tapping the Heart Rate icon.

After your Gear S2 takes your pulse for a few seconds, it shows you your current pulse and tells you whether your heart rate is within the average range for what you're doing.

This message appears for a few seconds and then the Heart Rate screen appears again, showing your most recent heart rate and how long ago you measured your heart rate. Below that information, you see what your heart rate was the last time you monitored it, along with how long ago that was.

FIGURE 9-10:
The summary entry in the list shows the exercise you did, for how long, and when you exercised.

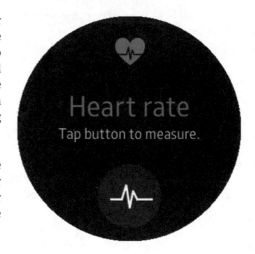

FIGURE 9-11:
The brown Heart Rate icon appears at the bottom of the screen.

Monitoring your water intake

Our bodies consist of between 50 and 75 percent water, depending on your age and gender, and staying hydrated is an essential key to good health, but people easily forget to get enough fluids. The S Health app allows you to record glasses of water you drink throughout the day so that you can look at the amount you drink at the end of the day and learn whether you need to drink more.

To track your water intake, from the Heart Rate screen, rotate the bezel to the right until you feel the bezel click. Now you can tell S Health when you've consumed a glass of water in the Water Tracker screen (see Figure 9-12). A glass of water contains eight ounces of the precious liquid. Just tap the Add icon after you've completely drained a glass of water (or some other fluid), not when you start drinking.

FIGURE 9-12:
Track your fluid intake. (Caffeinated fluids don't count!)

After you tap the Add icon at the bottom of the screen, the number of glasses in the screen goes up by one. If you want to see how many glasses of water you've consumed over a period of several days, tap the number of glasses on the Water Tracker screen.

When you tap the number of glasses, you see a graph that shows the number of glasses you've consumed today. Rotate the bezel to the left and right to see the number of glasses you've consumed in the past few days to see how consistent your water intake is. Return to the Water Tracker screen by pressing the Back button.

Getting too much caffeine?

Some of us (perhaps many of us) say that we can never have too much caffeine, but if you're someone who needs to keep track of your caffeine intake to ensure that you can sleep at night, you can do this in S Health. To track your caffeine intake, from the Water Tracker screen, rotate the bezel to the right until you feel the bezel click and you see the Caffeine Tracker screen (see Figure 9-13). Tap the Add icon after you've finished drinking a caffeinated beverage.

Accurately tracking your caffeine levels can be difficult because those levels vary from one caffeinated drink to another. However, S Health considers one caffeinated drink to be an eight-ounce brewed cup of coffee, which typically has 95 mg of caffeine. You may need to search the web or view the side of your caffeinated beverage bag or can to find out how much caffeine is in your drink; then tap the Add icon as many times as needed in the Caffeine Tracker screen.

For example, if you have a caffeinated beverage that has 300 mg of caffeine, you need to tap the Add icon on the Caffeine Tracker screen at least three

FIGURE 9-13:
Track your caffeine consumption.

times to convey a total of 285 mg. You may want to tap the Caffeine Tracker screen a fourth time if you consider the extra 15 mg to count as a fourth cup of coffee and thus remind yourself that you may want to cut back real soon now. (If everything you see is shaking, that's also a sign that you may want to cut back.)

If you want to see how many cups of coffee (or the equivalent caffeine amount) you've ingested over a period of several days, tap the number of cups on the Caffeine Tracker screen. You see a graph that shows the number of cups you've consumed today. Rotate the bezel to the left and right to see the number of cups you've consumed in the past few days. Return to the Caffeine Tracker screen by pressing the Back button.

Changing S Health Settings

You may want to change the S Health app settings before you start monitoring your health with the app. These settings include telling S Health more about you and your body, your goals, how you want the app to monitor your heart, get health alerts (or not), and get help about the app. You can also change the settings if something has changed recently, such as a reduction in your body weight because S Health is doing its job helping you get fit.

You change the S Health settings within the Settings screen. To get there, in the watch screen, press the Home button to open the Apps screen. If you're not on the first page of the Apps screen, swipe from left to right until you see the first page.

Then tap the S Health icon, which is at the 4 o'clock position on the screen. Within the S Health screen, rotate the bezel to the right until you see the Settings screen, shown in Figure 9-14. Now tap the Settings icon.

In the Settings menu screen (see Figure 9-15) that appears, you can swipe up and down to select one of five options:

» **Profile:** This option, which is selected when you first open the Settings menu screen, allows you to tell S Health more about yourself so that you can get more detailed recommendations about how to optimize your health based on your heart rate, fluid and caffeine intake, and exercise habits.

» **Step Target:** Allows you to change your daily step target goals.

» **Auto HR:** Lets you tell S Health whether to monitor your heart rate automatically and, if so, how often S Health should check your heart rate.

» **Alert:** Lets you turn various health alerts on and off.

» **Help:** Lets you get quick information about using the S Health app.

FIGURE 9-14:
The green Settings icon appears at the bottom of the screen.

FIGURE 9-15:
The Profile option is selected in the Settings screen by default.

Profile

Change profile settings by tapping Profile in the Settings menu screen. For reasons only Samsung knows, Samsung has default options for these settings, but you can change them easily. In the Profile screen, shown in Figure 9-16, swipe up and down and then tap one or more of the following settings:

>> **Gender:** By default, the gender is male. Tap this option to change between Male and Female.

>> **Date of Birth:** Enter your date of birth. The default date is January 1, 1980, which is most likely wrong, so you need to change it.

>> **Height:** Set your height, which by default is 5 feet, 6 inches.

>> **Weight:** Set your current weight, which is 143 pounds by default.

>> **Distance Unit:** Change the distance unit between mi (miles), which is the default, and km (kilometers).

FIGURE 9-16:
By default, the Gender option is selected in the Profile screen.

After you change your profile information, S Health modifies its recommendations for optimum health based on data for your specific gender, age group, height, and weight.

Step Target

The default target for the number of steps you take each day is 6,000. However, if you think this number is unrealistic based on your activity or circumstances, tap Step Target in the Settings menu screen. Then change the target in the Step Target screen, shown in Figure 9-17.

Change the target by rotating the bezel to the left and right to decrease and increase, respectively, the number of steps you think is doable each day. When you're done, tap Set to return to the Settings menu screen.

FIGURE 9-17:
Tap Set at the bottom of the screen above the tick marks.

Auto HR

S Health monitors your heart rate occasionally throughout the day. If you want S Health to monitor your heart rate more often, or don't want S Health to monitor your heart rate at all, tap Auto HR in the list (see Figure 9-18).

Swipe up and down in the screen shown in Figure 9-19 to view all three options, and select an option by tapping it:

>> **Frequent:** S Health monitors your heart rate frequently and alerts you with a notification if it thinks you have an issue that warrants your attention.

>> **Moderate:** This is the default option. The S Health app still alerts you with a notification if the app thinks you need to know about something.

>> **Off:** Turns off automatic heart rate monitoring. You can always monitor your heart rate automatically in the Heart Rate screen (see the "Measuring your heart rate" section, earlier in this chapter, for more details).

FIGURE 9-18:
The current Auto HR setting, Moderate, appears in green underneath the white Auto HR option text.

FIGURE 9-19:
The default selected option in the list is Moderate.

Alert

S Health alerts you with a notification when the app detects that one of three things have happened:

>> You have achieved your daily step target.

>> You are walking or running at a pace that S Health considers to be healthy for you.

>> You have been inactive for an hour and S Health thinks you need to get up and walk around before you ossify in your current spot.

Swipe up and down in the Alert screen, shown in Figure 9-20, to see that the Step Target Achieved, Healthy Pace, and Inactive Time alerts are all on. You can when each alerts is on because it has an On icon (a green circle with an I inside it) to the right of its name.

To turn off an alert, tap its name in the list. After you tap the alert name, the On icon changes to an Off icon, which is a gray circle with an O inside it. When you've finished making changes, return to the Settings menu screen by pressing the Back button.

FIGURE 9-20:
The Step Target alert is on.

Help

If you want more information about getting the most from S Health and how S Health tracks your activities, tap Help in the Settings menu screen. The Help screens don't provide as much information as this helpful book you're reading (and, I hope, enjoying), but it does provide some quick information that you can use to make decisions about using the S Health app.

Tap one of the six category options in the Help screen, shown in Figure 9-21, to get more information about each of these categories:

>> 24-Hr Activity Log

>> Steps

- » Exercise

- » Heart Rate

- » Water

- » Caffeine

After you read the information on the screen, you can return to the Help screen by pressing the Back button. Press the Back button two more times to return to the Settings screen. Then you can rotate the bezel to the left to view the other S Health screens such as the Heart Rate and the Track Your Steps screens.

FIGURE 9-21:
Tap 24-Hr Activity Log in the list to get quick information about your activity log.

The New Frontier

IN THIS PART . . .

Shopping for Gear S2 apps in the Samsung Galaxy Apps store on your smartphone

Downloading, installing, and running an app on your Gear S2

Finding Gear S2 app development websites and resources

Designing, developing, and distributing your Gear S2 app

Chapter 10

Go, Go Gear S2 Apps

The one thing that distinguishes a successful mobile product from one that's not so successful is the number of apps you can download from the manufacturer's app store. (Just ask Microsoft and its app issues with Windows Phone.) The Samsung Gear S2 has hundreds of apps available, with more being added each day.

When you have your Gear S2 connected to your smartphone using a Bluetooth or Wi-Fi connection, you can add a new Gear S2 app from Samsung's Galaxy Apps app on your smartphone, which is always on duty. After you find an app you want and download it, the Galaxy Apps store automatically installs the new Gear S2 app on your smartwatch so that you can start using it right away. Wowsers.

In this chapter, you learn how to shop for, download, and install a Gear S2 app from the Galaxy Apps store. Next, you discover how to launch your installed app on the Gear S2 and see how to view all the apps that are currently open within the Recent Apps screen. And in case you get an app that you don't like, you can find out in this chapter how to remove it.

TIP

Don't go looking for new apps for the Gear S2 in the Google Play Store app on your smartphone. The Google Play Store manages only Android apps, and your Gear S2 uses the Tizen operating system to run the smartwatch.

Installing a Shiny New App

Before you start installing a new app on your Gear S2, be sure your smartphone is also in plain sight. Then press the Home button on your Gear S2 to open the Apps screen. In the Apps screen, swipe from right to left (or rotate the bezel to the right) until you see the third and last page in the Apps screen. Then tap the Get More Apps icon, shown in Figure 10-1.

After you tap the icon, you see a message that asks you to download Gear S2 apps using your smartphone, as you see in Figure 10-2. The message disappears after a few seconds, and you see the third page of the Apps screen on your Gear S2 again.

FIGURE 10-1:
The Get More Apps icon is at the 11 o'clock position on the screen.

FIGURE 10-2:
Look at your smartphone to see the wonderful apps you can download.

Now turn your attention to your smartphone screen, which shows you the Samsung Gear Apps page within the Galaxy Apps app, shown in Figure 10-3. The screen shows you Samsung's featured picks for Gear S2 apps.

REMEMBER

Whenever you want to view a list of the most downloaded free apps, tap Top Free within the dark gray section bar that you see in Figure 10-4. The apps that are already installed on your Gear S2 appear at the top of the list.

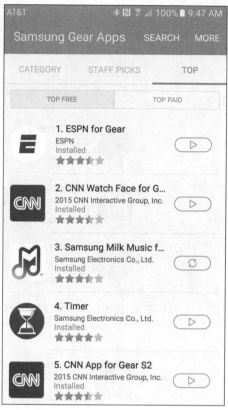

FIGURE 10-3:
Swipe up and down the screen to view all Samsung's picks for Gear S2 apps.

FIGURE 10-4:
Swipe up and down the list to view all apps in the Top Free category.

Below the tab bar are three section names in the section bar: Featured, Top Free, and Top Paid (see Figure 10-5). Samsung selected the Featured section by default, but if you want to see apps that won't cost you anything to download, tap Top Free. If you want to view apps that require you to pay a small fee to support the app developer, tap Top Paid.

If you have an idea of what type of app you want to download, swipe from left to right in the tab bar and then tap the Categories tab. The seven category tiles shown in Figure 10-6 appear, and you can tap a tile to see apps within that category.

For example, tap Utilities to view a list of apps in the Utilities category (see Figure 10-7). Samsung defines a utility as any other app that doesn't fit within any of the other six categories, kind of like a drawer filled with stuff that doesn't really go anywhere else in your house. Any utility app that is already installed, such as Stopwatch and the Flipboard News Briefing app, appears in the screen. Swipe up and down to view all the apps in the category.

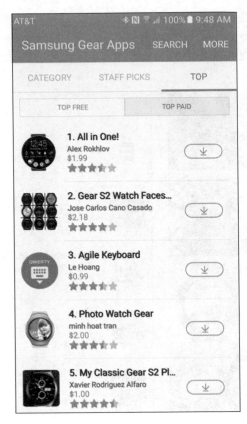

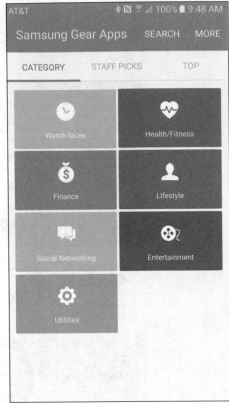

FIGURE 10-5:
Tap Top Paid if you want to see only the apps that you must pay for.

FIGURE 10-6:
Select an app from one of seven categories.

TIP

If you don't want to wade through all the apps to find the one you want, you can filter the list by tapping the Paid, Free, or New tabs within the tab bar. Figure 10-8 shows the Free in the tab bar, listing all the apps available for download at no charge.

Say that you're interested in installing the free Calculator app on your Gear S2 because, as we've been told (and sold) since at least the 1980s, what is a smartwatch without a calculator? Tap Calculator in the list to view the Details screen, shown in Figure 10-9. Within the Details screen, you can get more information about the app, including reviews from other Gear S2 users. If you decide to install it, tap the blue Install icon (see Figure 10-9) that appears under the rating stars in the Details screen.

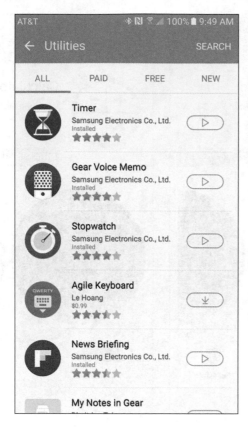

FIGURE 10-7:
Each app already installed on your Gear S2 has the word Installed below the developer name.

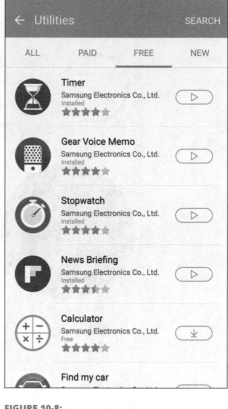

FIGURE 10-8:
Apps you have already installed appear at the top of the list within the Free section.

Your smartphone's app called Galaxy Apps downloads and installs it on the Gear S2 (all made possible by the Bluetooth or Wi-Fi connection between your smartphone and smartwatch). When the installation process is complete, start the app on your smartphone by tapping the Open icon on the smartphone screen, as shown in Figure 10-10. If you decide you don't want the app after all, tap the gray Uninstall icon.

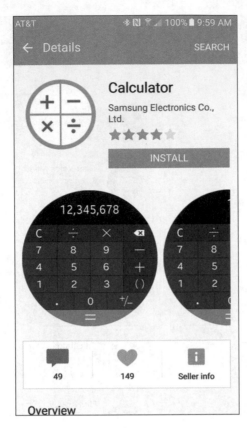

FIGURE 10-9:
The Install icon.

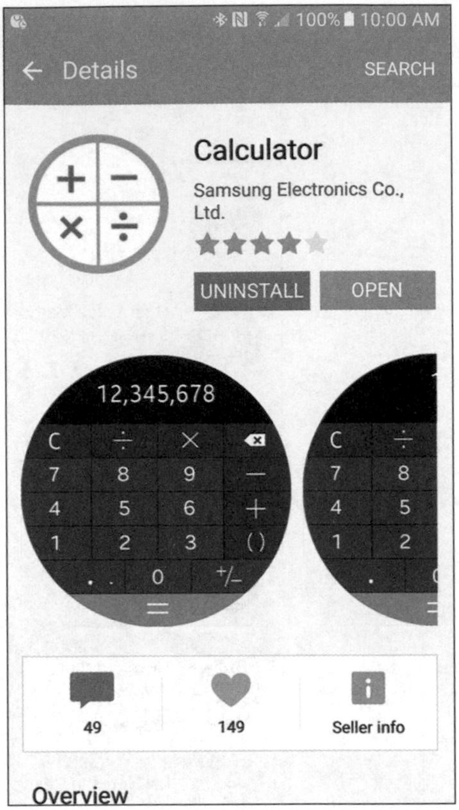

FIGURE 10-10:
Your app is ready to open on your smartphone.

Launching Your New App

After you tap the Open icon within the app's Details screen on your smartphone, the app screen appears on your Gear S2. (See Figure 10-11, which in this case shows the newly installed Calculator app screen.) You're not going to become Calculon when you use this Calculator app because it's a basic calculator that just lets you make some quick calculations. To start calculating, just tap the appropriate icons and view the calculated result in the black area at the top of the screen.

If you don't need the app at the moment, press the Back button to view the Apps screen. Note that the Gear S2 has created a fourth page of apps within the Apps screen because the first three pages are already filled with preinstalled apps. The new app is the only installed app on this new page at the moment (see Figure 10-12).

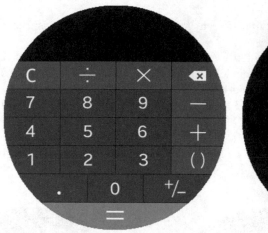

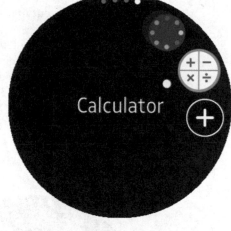

FIGURE 10-11:
Your new app displays on your Gear S2 after you've installed it using your smartphone.

FIGURE 10-12:
The new app's icon appears at the 2 o'clock position on the fourth Apps screen page.

You can close the Galaxy Apps app on your smartphone unless you want to download another app.

Viewing Your Recent Apps

When you're in an app and you press the Back button within the app's home screen to return to the Apps screen (or press the Home button to view the watch screen), you may think you're closing the app. In reality, you're only minimizing the app while another app or the watch face appears on your Gear S2 screen.

To open an app you've minimized, you can either tap the app's icon within the Apps screen or tap the app's image within the Recent Apps screen. You access the Recent Apps screen in one of two ways:

>> If you're in the watch screen, press the Home button and then tap the Recent Apps icon (see Figure 10-13).

>> If you're in an Apps screen page other than the first page, swipe from left to right (or rotate the bezel to the left) until you see the first Apps page on the screen. Now tap the Recent Apps icon.

Within the Recent Apps screen, you see an image of the most recent app you used.

Swipe from right to left to view all the apps you've minimized. When you reach the last app, swipe from left to right to go to the app you want to open. Of course, you can also rotate your bezel from left to right until you find the app you want to open. When you find the app you want to open, tap its image in the center of the screen.

You can close the app by tapping the Close icon in the upper-right corner of the image (see Figure 10-14).

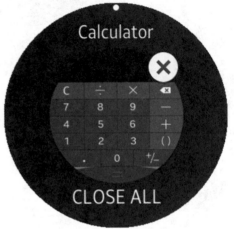

FIGURE 10-13:
The Recent Apps icon appears at the 1 o'clock position on the screen.

FIGURE 10-14:
The Close icon is a white circle with a red *X* inside it.

TIP

If you close all the open apps, you'll free some memory space on your Gear S2. To do so, tap Close All at the bottom of the Recent Apps screen.

Doing Away with Apps

Cleaning out your computing devices of unnecessary programs, files, and messages now and then is always good. If you include the Gear S2 as part of that data scrub, you can uninstall some apps — which is as easy as saying "Go, go gadget delete apps."

To delete an app, follow these steps:

1. In the watch screen, press the Home button to open the Apps screen.

2. Swipe to the page that contains the app you want to delete.

3. Tap and hold your finger in the center of the screen until it shows the words *Edit Mode;* the Delete icon (a white circle with a red minus sign) appears at one side of the app's icon, as shown in Figure 10-15.

4. Tap the Delete icon.

The Uninstall screen, shown in Figure 10-16, appears.

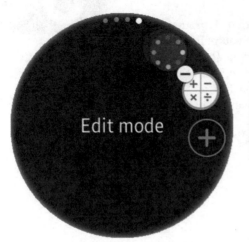

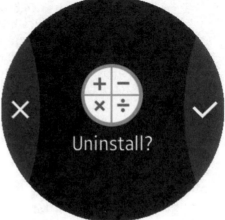

FIGURE 10-15:
The Delete icon is a red minus sign inside a white circle.

FIGURE 10-16:
Keep the Calculator app installed by tapping the Cancel icon on the left side of the screen.

5. Tap the Confirm (with the check mark) icon on the right side of the screen.

Tap Cancel if you want to keep the app after all.

The Apps screen appears in Edit Mode without your uninstalled app showing on it. If your app was the only one on an App screen page, that entire page disappears and you see what is now the last page in the Apps screen.

When you're in Edit Mode, you can see which apps you can uninstall by looking for the Delete icon included with the app icon. For example, Figure 10-17 shows that you can uninstall the Milk Music app but not the Gallery app.

There are quite a few apps that can't be uninstalled. That's because they're either vital to the functionality of the Gear S2, such as Settings, or because Samsung thinks those apps are too important to delete. With the Gallery app, for example, Samsung wants you to share photos from your smart-phone on your Gear S2 so that you can show other people the photos — and show off the watch to a potential buyer.

If you want to find other apps that you can uninstall while you're in Edit Mode, swipe left and right (or rotate the bezel left and right) to view other Apps screen pages. You can get out of Edit Mode by pressing the Back button.

FIGURE 10-17:
The Delete icons appear in the upper-right corners of the app icons.

Chapter 11

Thinking of Building an App? (Yes, You Can!)

Plenty of apps available for the Gear S2, and more are being added every day. Even so, maybe you can't find an app that does what you need it to do, or maybe you think an existing app could be better. If a little voice in your head starts crowding out your other thoughts (hopefully not to the degree as when Homer Simpson learned about Krusty's Clown College), Samsung makes it easy for you to develop an app and then post it on Samsung's Seller Office so that you can make a happy buck or two.

Gear S2 development could fill up a book of its own, and app development is well beyond the scope of this book. However, this short chapter does give you an overview of how to get started on using Samsung's tools to design and distribute your very own app.

In this chapter, I point you toward the development websites for both the Gear S2 and the Tizen operating system and where to acquaint yourself with the required design standards for the Gear S2 screen. You also see how to download the Tizen Software Development Kit and view sample projects. Finally, this chapter gives you tips on distributing and managing your app in the Samsung Seller Office.

Finding the Right Development Sites

The Samsung Developer website for the Gear S2 is the first place to go when you have the itch to develop an app. The website, which is located at `http://developer.samsung.com/gear`, contains three icons on the home page, shown in Figure 11-1, that take you step-by-step through creating an app for Gear S2 users.

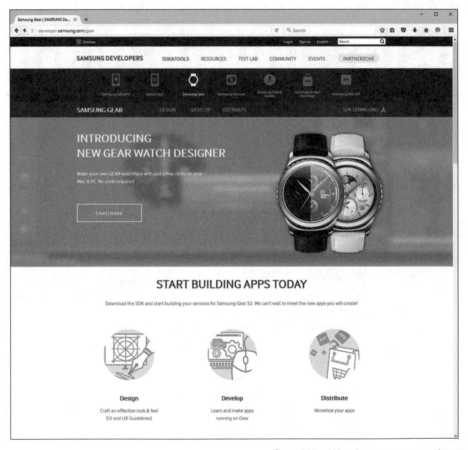

FIGURE 11-1:
Look for the three step-by-step icons under the Start Building Apps Today section on the page.

Source: `http://developer.samsung.com/gear`

You can find a related Samsung website for wearable technologies at `http://developer.samsung.com/wearable/`, but this website is more generalized, and I don't cover it in this chapter. You can check it out at your leisure.

Another good resource is the Tizen development website at `https://developer.tizen.org/`. On this website, shown in Figure 11-2, you can get information about different devices that use the Tizen operating system, including wearable devices. You can also join the Tizen User Community to ask and answer questions.

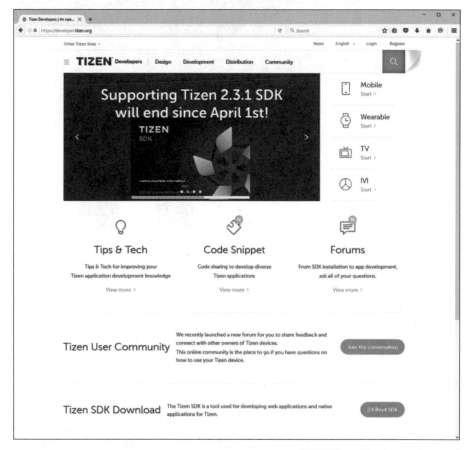

FIGURE 11-2:
The Tizen developer website is chock-full of tips, shared code, and information from fellow developers.

Source: `https://developer.tizen.org/`

Designing an App

After you've reviewed the Samsung and Tizen websites and you've convinced yourself that yes, you can build it, click Design in the Samsung Developer site for the Gear S2 (refer to Figure 11-1). The Home Structure and Rich Notifications links shown in Figure 11-3 are the ones you want to click to get the design guidelines you need. (If you're curious about the Gear Watch Designer app, flip to Chapter 14 to find out more about it.)

FIGURE 11-3:
The Home
Structure
and Rich
Notification
links appear
within the
Spotlight
section on
the page.

Source: *http://developer.samsung.com/gear/design*

Click the Home Structure link to get a tutorial about how the user interface elements work together on Gear to create a great experience for users. When you finish reading the tutorial, return to the Design page and then click Rich Notification shown in Figure 11-3 so that you can learn how notification design on the Gear S2 works.

You may want to play around with a few apps on your Gear S2 as you read these tutorials on your computer or smartphone so that you can reinforce the concepts covered in the tutorials.

TIP

Developing an App

When you have a basic sense of how to design an app, it's time for the fun part: creating the app. On the Samsung Developer website (`http://developer.samsung.com/gear`), click Develop in the menu bar near the top of the page. The Develop page displays three links in the middle of the page (see Figure 11-4): Getting Started, Download SDKs, and Sample Projects.

FIGURE 11-4:
The blue menu bar is the only royal blue bar on the page, so it's easy to find.

Source: http://developer.samsung.com/gear/develop

Hello, world!

If you're new to the world of the Tizen operating system, click Getting Started (or its associated icon) in the Develop page (refer to Figure 11-4). The Getting Started page, shown in Figure 11-5, gives you a good introduction to development for both native applications and Companion applications. Companion applications are like

Doctor Who's companion: An Android smartphone needs to come along with the Gear S2 and interact with the Gear S2 app to get stuff done.

Source: http://developer.samsung.com/gear/develop/getting-started

You can create apps either using web technologies, including HTML5, CSS, and JavaScript, or using the C programming language to create native apps. Native apps use features specific to the use of your Gear S2, such as a heart rate sensor. You can develop an app using either the web or C programming methods with the Tizen Software Development Kit (SDK).

Scroll down on the page to view links that help you develop your first web or native application, such as the following:

>> **Set Up SDK:** Learn how to install the SDK and get further resources.

>> **Create a Project:** Get a basic introduction to creating your web or native app project.

>> **Build an App:** Learn how to build an app automatically and manually in the SDK.

>> **Run an App:** Understand how to run your built app from within the SDK.

>> **Create a Simple UI:** Find out how to program a simple user interface for your Gear S2.

What's more, the Develop page offers a section called "Create Your Watch Face" that contains links that help you create your own watch face. When you scroll down to the bottom of the page, you also find sections with links for developing web and native Companion apps.

REMEMBER

So which technology is right for you? If you want your app to make the most of the features and functionality of the Gear S2, develop a native app. If you want your app to be available on a wider variety of smartwatches that run the Tizen OS, develop a web app.

Turning on debugging and Wi-Fi

Before you start using the Tizen SDK, you need to set up your Gear S2 to turn on the debugging service so that the SDK can fix any bugs with your app code.

Here's how to turn on debugging on your Gear S2:

1. Open the Settings screen.

2. Within the Settings screen, swipe up on the screen until you see Gear Info.

3. Tap Gear Info.

4. Swipe up on the screen until you see Debugging.

5. Tap Debugging.

6. In the confirmation screen that appears, tap the blue Confirmation button on the right side of the screen.

Now the Debugging feature is on (see in Figure 11-6).

FIGURE 11-6:
You know the Debugging feature is on because a green On icon appears to the right of the word Debugging.

You also have to turn on Wi-Fi on your Gear S2. Both the Gear S2 and the computer you're using (and it has to be a computer, as you see in the next section) have to use the same wireless network for the SDK and your smartwatch to communicate. Don't remember how to set up Wi-Fi on your Gear S2? Just bookmark this page and go back to Chapter 3. I'll take a break and be back when you're done.

Getting the SDK

On the Develop page at `http://developer.samsung.com/gear` (refer to Figure 11-4), click Download SDKs or its associated icon within the Spotlight section on the page. The Tizen SDK page appears, as shown in Figure 11-7, so that you can download either the standard SDK, which is the SDK with a graphic user interface, or the command-line SDK, which allows you to type in commands onscreen to perform tasks.

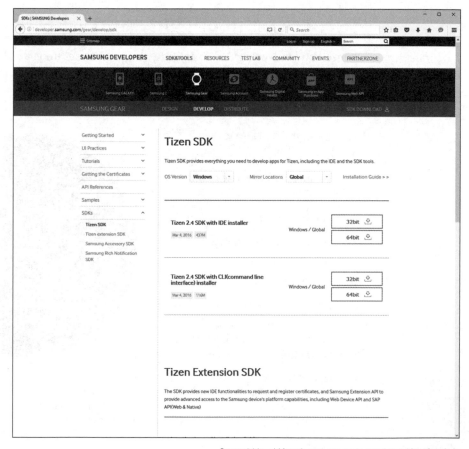

FIGURE 11-7:
The settings bar appears below the Tizen SDK heading and contains the OS Version and Mirror Locations drop-down lists.

Source: *http://developer.samsung.com/gear/develop/sdk*

Unless you really like typing in commands and are willing to learn all the commands you need to type to run the command-line SDK, or you're a pretty good developer, it's probably better to stick with (and enjoy) the high-powered automatic everything included in the standard SDK.

The default operating system for the SDK is Windows. You can use the SDK in Windows 7, Windows 8, or Windows 10. Windows also comes in either 32-bit or 64-bit flavors, and you need to know which flavor you have installed on your computer. (Don't know? I tell you how to find out in the Technical Stuff paragraph at the end of this section.) Then you can download the 32-bit or 64-bit version of the SDK that runs with your flavor of Windows.

If you don't have Windows, no sweat. Tizen makes its SDK available for the Mac OS and Ubuntu Linux operating systems as well. (If you have a distribution of Linux that's not Ubuntu, you're on the outs.)

Just below the Tizen SDKs heading at the top of the page shown in Figure 11-7, you see the settings row with the OS Version as Windows and the Mirror Locations as Global. Click the down arrow to the right of Windows and then select Ubuntu Linux or Mac OS X from the drop-down list. When you select Ubuntu Linux, you can also download either the 32-bit or 64-bit version of the SDK.

If you're in Brazil, China, or India and you want to download the SDK from a local server (and thus get faster service), click the down arrow to the right of Global and then select your country from the drop-down list.

If you aren't sure whether your version of Windows or Ubuntu is 32-bit or 64-bit, check your system information in the appropriate Control Panel. If you download the 64-bit SDK and you have a 32-bit system, you'll learn about your Windows system the hard way when you find that the 64-bit SDK version won't install on your computer.

Installing the SDK

After you select the operating system (and mirror location, if necessary), the two installer sections appear below the settings bar. Within the Tizen 2.4 SDK with IDE Installer section, download the Tizen SDK by clicking the appropriate button. For example, to install the SDK for 64-bit Windows, click the 64-bit button.

The helpful and patient installation process takes you through the installation process and then through the upgrade process to ensure that every component in the SDK is up-to-date. When you're finished, you see the SDK window on your computer screen, as shown in Figure 11-8.

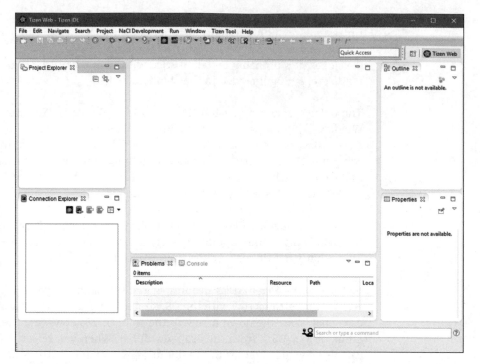

FIGURE 11-8:
The Tizen SDK
window is
divided into
a number of
different panes
to report all
the informa-
tion you need
as you develop
your app.

Reviewing sample projects

If this is your first time using the Tizen SDK, review the information within the Getting Started page that I describe in the "Hello, world!" section earlier in this chapter.
That page has links to step-by-step instructions for creating an app in the SDK.

The SDK also has a large number of sample projects for your perusal for both web
and native apps. Here's how to open the list of sample projects for a native app:

1. **Click File in the menu bar.**

2. **Hover the mouse over New.**

    A secondary drop-down menu appears to the right of the primary drop-down
    menu.

3. **Click Project in the secondary drop-down menu.**

    The New Project window opens and the Tizen Native Project option in the list is
    selected by default.

4. **Click Next.**

    The New Tizen Native Project window appears, as shown in Figure 11-9.

FIGURE 11-9:
The New Tizen Native Project is chock-full of templates and samples you can use to build your project.

5. **Click the Online Sample icon.**

A list of online sample projects appears in the samples list on the left side of the screen, and the (Tutorial) Account Manager sample is selected by default. The project description appears to the right of the selected sample in the list.

6. **Scroll up and down in the sample list on the left side of the screen and then click the sample project you want to open.**

As you scroll up and down the list, you notice an icon to the right of the sample name. Samples with a rectangular smartphone icon are samples designed for a smartphone. Samples with a circular watch icon are samples designed for a smartwatch. Mr. Spock would say that it is logical to find a sample project that has a smartwatch icon next to it in the list.

What's more, you should find a sample name that has "(Circle)" before the actual name of the sample because this means that the sample is designed for a circular watch, such as the Gear S2. If you're not sure whether the sample is designed for a circular smartwatch, look in the description to the right of the list. The description contains a screenshot, and if the screenshot for your smartwatch sample is circular, you know that the sample you've selected is designed for the Gear S2.

7. **Click Finish.**

The project information appears in the Project Explorer pane tree, which is on the left side of the Tizen SDK window (refer to Figure 11-8). You can navigate through the tree to open folders and view files within them. Double-click a file to view the project information within the various panes in the Tizen SDK window.

Distributing Your App

After you've developed, debugged, and polished your app to the point where you think it's ready for sale, you can take the final step in your development journey: Distributing your app.

This is Samsung's show, which means that you can distribute your Gear S2 app only on Samsung's Seller Office app store. You start the distribution process by going to the Samsung Developer website (http://developer.samsung.com/gear) for the Gear S2 and then clicking Distribute in the blue menu bar near the top of the page (refer to Figure 11-3). The three icons on the Distribute screen, shown in Figure 11-10, are links that enable you to learn more about distributing your app.

To learn about distributing your app, the main link that you need is the How to Distribute link. Click that link to bring up the How to Distribute screen shown in Figure 11-11.

Validation is occasionally good in life, and it's a requirement for your Gear S2 app. Validating your app means that you're testing your app to ensure that it meets Samsung's standards for usability, functionality, compatibility, and content. (For example, apps cannot include information about illegal activities.) In the Prerequisites section at the top of the screen, click View Details after each subsection to get more information about each subsection topic, such as Samsung's checklist for app quality.

Distributing your great apps

With a reach to all users in over 180 countries, the Samsung Gear Apps is a specifically designed apps store for Gear apps.

Spotlight

How to Distribute

Find a comprehensive walkthrough on using the Seller Office. Add your app, promote, and even manage it yourself.

Samsung Gear Apps

A One-Stop-Shop for all the apps you need for the Gear.

Samsung Seller Office

Your portal to sell, manage, and promote your applications and even, Gear Apps.

FIGURE 11-10: Click these links to see how to distribute your app, use Samsung Gear Apps, and use Samsung Seller Office.

Source: http://developer.samsung.com/gear/distribute

Creating a Seller Office account

After you've reviewed the checklist and policies for validating Gear S2 apps on the How to Distribute page, you can swipe down the screen to learn how to create a Seller Office account (see Figure 11-12).

You may notice that all instances of the words Seller Office in this section are text links. Click one of the links to open the Seller Office website in another tab on your web browser and go through the process of creating your account.

TIP

Consider bookmarking the Seller Office website after you open it in a new browser tab so that you can go back to the site just by clicking the bookmark in your browser.

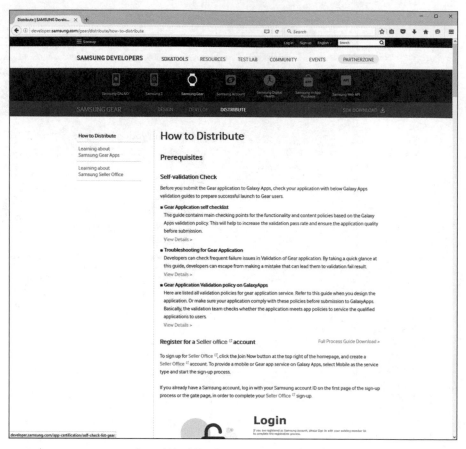

FIGURE 11-11:
The View Details link appears after the subsection text.

Source: *http://developer.samsung.com/gear/distribute/how-to-distribute*

Registering your app

To register your app, go to `http://developer.samsung.com/gear/distribute` and click the How to Distribute icon to open the How to Distribute page. Scroll down the page until you see the Register a Gear App section, shown in Figure 11-13.

Scroll down the screen to get step-by-step instructions for registering an app. Within these instructions, you find out how to complete the following tasks:

>> Enter your app information as well as the category (or categories) so that shoppers can find your app more easily. You can select from up to two categories. You can also select a subcategory within each category.

>> Upload and register your app binary file.

>> Set the country of origin and price of your app as well as request commercial seller status if you want to sell your app. You may want to check competing

app prices to be competitive, or charge a price you think is fair. No matter what you charge, pay close attention to the latest terms and conditions of pricing your app.

» Submit a verification request to Samsung.

Source: http://developer.samsung.com/gear/distribute/how-to-distribute

FIGURE 11-12: Under a screenshot of the Seller Account website, you find instructions for how to create an account.

After Samsung has verified your app, the app becomes available to others. To find it, open the Galaxy Apps app, search for your app, and then giggle uncontrollably when you find it in the category you specified.

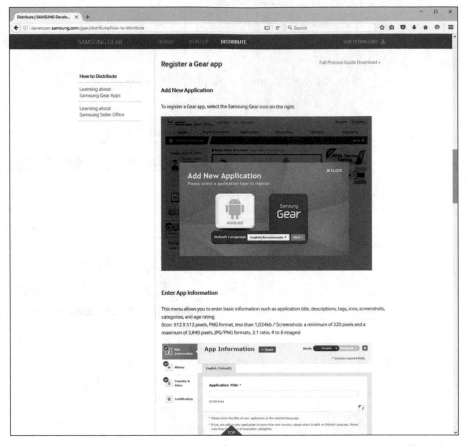

FIGURE 11-13:
The Register
a Gear App
section comes
complete
with helpful
screenshots.

Source: http://developer.samsung.com/gear/distribute

Becoming the overseer of your Seller Office account

While you wait for Samsung to verify your app, you may want to brush up on how to manage your Samsung Seller Office account. Here's how to log into your account:

1. Go to http://seller.samsungapps.com/ in your web browser.

2. Click Log In in the upper-right corner of the screen.

3. In the Log In window that appears, type the email account and password associated with the account.

4. Click the Log In button.

Easy, no? Now you can check to see whether your app has been validated by Samsung. When it has, you can view information about how your app is selling.

You can find a nice tutorial by Samsung about managing your Seller Office account. Go to the Distribute page at `http://developer.samsung.com/gear/distribute` (refer to Figure 11-10) and click the Samsung Seller Office icon to open the Learning About Samsung Seller Office page, shown in Figure 11-14.

FIGURE 11-14: Each section on the page includes a screenshot to illustrate what's being discussed within the section.

Source: `http://developer.samsung.com/gear/distribute/learn-about-seller-office`

Scroll down for info on managing the following information:

>> **Add New Application:** Add a new app to be validated by Samsung. You can submit as many apps as you want.

>> **Buyer Comments:** View buyer comments about your app. You can also reply to each comment if you want.

>> **Applications:** Check the verification status of apps, update your validated apps, apply price discounts, and stop selling your apps.

>> **Accounting:** See how many monetary bills you'll collect from your sales. You also see how many of those bills have pictures of Washington and how many have pictures of Franklin.

>> **Statistics:** Review how many users have downloaded your app and the countries in which your app has sold.

>> **Assistance:** Get help with using Seller Office and ask the Seller Office staff for help.

Log into Seller Office at any time and try these features for yourself.

Heal Your Gear

4

IN THIS PART . . .

Troubleshooting common problems with the Gear S2

Calling Samsung for more help

Finding support for the Tizen operating system that runs the Gear S2

Getting support from data carriers

Visiting website communities for support

Chapter 12

Troubleshooting and Getting Help

Your Gear S2 is a fine piece of machinery, but it's still a contraption created by human beings, so it may give you grief now and then. Perhaps you're running into a problem now and that's why you're reading this chapter. If so, or if you're just curious about how to resolve common problems with the Gear S2, this chapter tells you how to solve some of those problems — or at least offers some ideas for doing so.

Topics covered in this chapter include unfreezing your frozen Gear S2, resolving issues turning the Gear S2 on, fixing a sluggish touch screen, managing connectivity issues with Bluetooth, and checking issues with Gear Manager. If none of those solutions help, you may have to contact Samsung and take your Gear S2 out for servicing if Samsung decides that's what you need.

Unfreezing Your Gear S2

What can you do when your Gear S2 isn't working well and is freezing for periods of time before it starts working again? The problem may be that you have many apps running and sucking up all your smartwatch's resources. Or the performance of your Gear S2 may have been affected after you started running a particular app.

Try closing one or more open apps. You can do this in the watch screen by pressing the Home button to open the Apps screen. Then tap the Recent Apps icon, which is at about the 1 o'clock position in the Apps screen. Next, swipe back and forth until you find the app that you think may be causing the problem, and then tap the Close icon shown in Figure 12-1.

If your Gear S2 has frozen solid even after you've been patient and done something else for a while before checking it again, press and hold the Home button for seven seconds until you see the very tiny word *rebooting* in blue text in the upper-left corner

FIGURE 12-1:
The Close icon is a white circle with a red *X* inside it.

of the screen. Your Gear S2 reboots and should start up again without running any of the apps you had open before you had problems.

Back up and reset your Gear

If you're still having problems running your Gear S2 after you close all your apps or reboot your system, try resetting your smartwatch to its original factory specs so that it operates the same way as it did when you took it out of the box. But first, you need to back up your data, as explained next.

Backing up with Gear Manager

Before you reset your smartwatch, you should back up data on your Gear S2 because a factory reset deletes all data on your smartwatch. You can back up data on Gear Manager by following these easy–peasy steps:

1. **On your smartphone, open the Gear Manager app.**

    If you're not as familiar with Gear Manager as you'd like to be, bookmark this page, read Chapter 4, and then return here with newfound confidence.

2. **Tap Settings in the Gear Manager screen.**

The Settings screen opens and displays a list of settings you can change.

3. **Tap Back Up and Restore.**

The Back Up and Restore screen appears so that you can back up Gear S2 data to your smartphone and restore backup data to your Gear S2.

4. **Tap Back Up Data.**

The Gear Manager app backs up your data. When the app is done, the date and time you last backed up your Gear S2 appears under the Back Up Data setting title on the screen.

Resetting to factory specs

To reset to the original factory specifications (after having first backed up your data on your Gear S2), follow these steps:

1. **Press the Home button and then tap the Settings icon in the Apps screen that appears.**

The Settings icon is at the 7 o'clock position on the screen.

2. **In the Settings screen, swipe up in the screen or rotate the bezel to the right until you see Gear Info in the list, and tap it.**

The Gear Info screen opens.

3. **Swipe up in the screen (or rotate the bezel to the right) until you see Reset Gear, and tap it.**

The Reset Gear screen opens.

4. **Swipe up in the screen or (you know the refrain) rotate the bezel to the right until you see Factory Reset, as shown in Figure 12-2.**

5. **Tap Factory Reset.**

6. **Tap the Confirm icon on the right side of the Reset Gear screen to begin the reset process.**

All your settings and data you had on the Gear S2 are deleted.

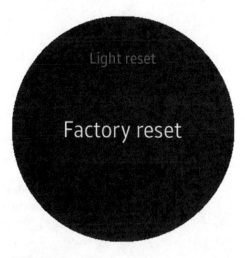

FIGURE 12-2:
Remove all data on the Gear S2 by tapping Factory Reset.

Now you can find out whether the problem persists. You may want to add apps back on your watch one at a time to see whether the problem reoccurs after you install an app. If you're still having problems, declare a red alert and skip ahead to the "Calling Samsung for Help" section in this chapter because it's time for you to call Samsung Command. (Yes, I'm trying to be funny. The real name is Samsung Customer Service.)

Resolving Issues with Getting Your Gear to Turn On

If you press the Home button for two or three seconds and don't feel the familiar vibration and see the Samsung Gear S2 screen, your battery may be out of juice. If that's not the problem, you need to replace either your battery or your charger.

You can find out whether your battery needs to be recharged by placing the Gear S2 on its charging dock, ensuring that the charging dock is plugged in, and then checking to see whether the charging light on your charger comes on. If it doesn't, you know the problem is in one of three places:

- >> **Your charger:** In this case, you need to call Samsung. (See the "Calling Samsung for Help" section, later in this chapter, for contact details.)
- >> **Your surge protector:** Try plugging the charger directly into a wall outlet. If your charger works, your surge protector is on the blink.
- >> **Your wall outlet:** Try plugging your charger into a different outlet.

If the charging light comes on, go de-stress by doing something else for an hour or so while the watch recharges, at least partially. When you remove the watch from the charger, you should see the battery charge percentage on the screen for a couple of seconds. If you don't see this charge percentage, push the Power button on the Gear S2 anyway and see whether it comes on.

If the Gear S2 still doesn't start, you're at the "Houston, we have a problem" stage of the diagnostic process and you need to call Hous . . . er, Samsung at the phone number I give you in the "Calling Samsung for Help" section later in this chapter.

Fixing a Sluggish Touch Screen

Your Gear S2 screen is small, so you can easily tap the wrong icon when using it. But what can you do when the touch screen still isn't working properly, such as when you swipe the screen and it takes longer than expected to move to the next screen or doesn't move at all? Here are some possible causes:

» **You have wet or unclean hands.** Your Gear S2 won't work as well if it can't detect the touch of your finger very well. If you have dirty hands, or if you washed them but didn't dry your fingers well, you may need to thoroughly wash and dry your fingers before you start using your fingers to operate your smartwatch.

» **Your software may be out of date.** Check the current Tizen OS version in the Gear Manager app on your smartphone. (See the "Checking Your Gear Manager" section later in this chapter to find out how to check Gear Manager for this information.)

» **You have a protective cover that isn't sticking properly to the screen, or the cover is damaged.** You can get a protective screen, such as the one from ArmorSuit (http://www.armorsuit.com), that helps shield the Gear S2 from smudgy fingers and scratches. If the shield itself isn't adhered to the screen properly, you may need to take the shield off and reattach it to the screen. Your shield may also have too many scratches and needs to be replaced.

Another way to test your touchscreen's responsiveness is to rotate the bezel as much as possible. If the touchscreen is sluggish even when you use the bezel, that could indicate that you have a more serious problem. It's time to skip ahead to the "Calling Samsung for Help" section to see how to contact Samsung.

Getting Bluetooth to Connect

If your smartphone can't connect to your Gear S2, it could be for one of the following reasons:

» Either your smartphone or your Gear S2 is currently off and you need to turn the device on.

» The Bluetooth service is off on one of your devices and you need to turn it on.

» What you've got here is a failure to communicate because your smartphone and Gear S2 are more than 32 feet (10 meters) away from each other. So get your devices closer and then see whether the devices will connect. If they don't and you think both devices are close enough to each other, open the Gear Manager app on your smartphone, tap More at the right side of the orange menu bar at the top of the screen, and then tap Connect in the pop-up menu that appears.

» If your devices are on, Bluetooth is enabled on your devices, and your devices are close, you may need to turn your smartphone or your Gear S2 off and then on again to finally convince one device that the other device exists.

If you're not sure that your Gear S2 Bluetooth service is on, here's how to check it on your smartwatch:

1. **Press the Home button to open the Apps screen.**

2. **Tap the Settings icon, which is at the 7 o'clock position on the Apps screen.**

   The Setting screen appears.

3. **Swipe up in the Settings screen or rotate the bezel to the right until you see the Connections options in the center of the screen.**

4. **Tap Connections.**

   The Connection screen appears.

5. **Tap Bluetooth.**

6. **If Bluetooth isn't on, tap Bluetooth in the Bluetooth screen, shown in Figure 12-3.**

After you turn on Bluetooth, the word Visible appears in blue under the Gear S2 name and Bluetooth ID (see Figure 12-3). You may also need to check your smartphone's Bluetooth setting.

Here's another suggestion if you've implemented all these suggestions and Bluetooth still doesn't work: Find another Bluetooth device that your smartphone can normally connect to, such as a headset or a printer. If your smartphone can connect to another Bluetooth device, you know the problem isn't with your smartphone.

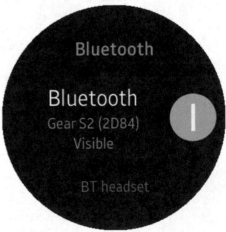

FIGURE 12-3:
You know Bluetooth is on because you see the green On icon on the screen.

In that case, perform a factory reset on your Gear S2 (see the "Unfreezing Your Gear S2" section, earlier in this chapter). Removing all apps and settings may also remove your Bluetooth problem, at which point you can reinstall each app and setting one at a time and try to determine what app or setting causes Bluetooth to stop working.

Checking Your Gear Manager

You should make sure that you have the latest version of your Tizen operating system installed, especially if you perform a factory reset of your Gear S2. The version of Tizen may have been updated since the time it was installed at the Samsung factory.

To check your Tizen version, grab your smartphone and follow these steps:

1. **Open the Gear Manager app on your smartphone.**

2. **Tap the Settings option in the Gear Manager home screen, shown in Figure 12-4.**

3. **Swipe down on the screen until you see the App Version option at the bottom of the list (see Figure 12-5); tap App Version.**

   You see both the version of the Samsung Gear driver for your smartphone and the Gear Plugin version, as shown in Figure 12-6. A *driver* is an app that tells your smartphone how to work with the Gear S2, and the Gear Plugin version is the version of the Gear Manager app itself.

   Samsung is very good about updating the Gear Manager app and implements an update as soon as it's available and transmitted to your smartphone. You know that the update has been installed when you see the notification on your smartphone.

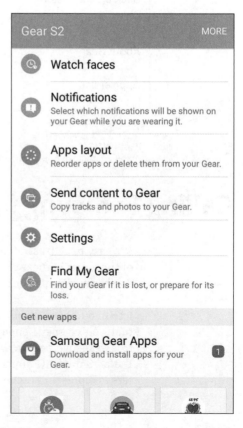

FIGURE 12-4:
The Settings icon is the fifth option in the list.

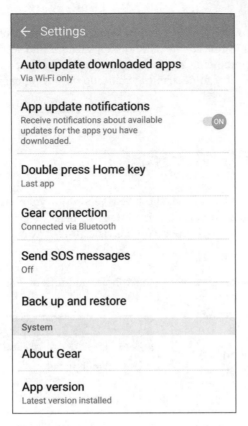

FIGURE 12-5:
The App Version option says the latest version is installed, but tap App Version to make sure.

FIGURE 12-6:
The version number for the Gear Plugin appears under the Gear Plugin name in the list.

Calling Samsung for Help

It's easy to be frustrated if you've tried all the suggestions in this chapter or none of the topics in these chapters match the problem you have. But today's your lucky day because you're not alone, and help is as close as your phone.

I tell you about plenty of online resources in Chapter 13, but if you've decided that you've spent enough time searching around online and you'd rather talk to a real, live person who will be happy to help you, you can call Samsung at 1-800-SAMSUNG. If you don't adhere to the somewhat archaic form of using letters to represent numbers when you dial a phone number, that's 1-800-726-7864.

Write down the Tizen software version

The Samsung customer support representative will likely need to know the version of the Tizen operating system that you have on your phone. Here's how to find it:

1. **On the watch screen, press the Home button to open the Apps screen.**

2. **Tap the Settings icon, which is at the 7 o'clock position on the Apps screen.**

3. **Swipe up in the Settings screen or rotate the bezel until you see Gear Info.**

4. **Tap Gear Info to open the Gear Info screen.**

5. **Tap About Device.**

6. **Swipe up in the screen or rotate the bezel until you see Software Version in the center of the screen shown in Figure 12-7.**

Bluetooth address

Software version
R732XXU2BPA4

Serial number

FIGURE 12-7:
The version number appears in blue underneath the Software Version text.

Turning off Reactivation Lock

If you read Chapter 4 and turned on Reactivation Lock, Samsung requires that you turn Reactivation Lock off before you send the Gear S2 back for service. Here's how to turn off Reactivation Lock in the Samsung Gear app on your smartphone:

1. **In the Gear Manager app home screen, tap Find My Gear, shown in Figure 12-8.**

2. **Tap Reactivation Lock in the Find My Gear screen (see Figure 12-9).**

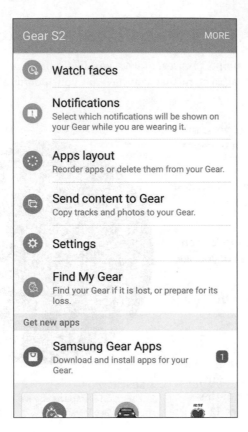

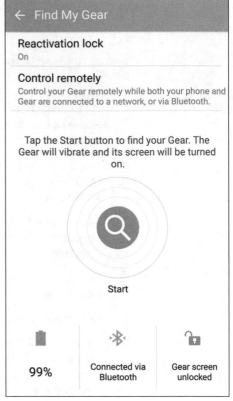

FIGURE 12-8:
The Find My Gear option is the only option with a green icon to the left of the option name.

FIGURE 12-9:
The Reactivation Lock option appears just below the orange menu bar at the top of the screen.

3. **Tap On in the Reactivation Lock screen (see Figure 12-10).**

The Samsung Account window appears (see Figure 12-11), asking for your account password.

4. **Type your password and then tap Confirm.**

Now Reactivation Lock is off. When the Samsung representative asks you to turn off Reactivation Lock, you can cheerfully tell the rep that you already did that, and you and the rep can focus on fixing your Gear S2.

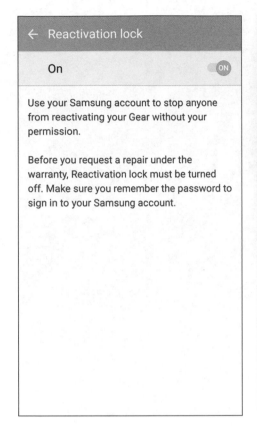

FIGURE 12-10:
The On option appears at the top of the screen just below the orange menu bar.

FIGURE 12-11:
After you type your password, the Confirm option appears in blue in the lower-right corner of the window.

Chapter 13

Sourcing More Help: The Support Is Out There

I n Chapter 12, I give you some tips and contact info for calling Samsung customer support in case you're having problems with your Gear S2. If you're looking for more support online, either to solve a problem or to get the most from your smartwatch, you can find plenty of online support at the tap of the finger (or a click of the mouse, if you prefer).

In this chapter, I tell you about about online support options from Samsung and Tizen, the creator of the operating system used by the Gear S2. You also find out where to find help if you purchased your smartwatch from one of the three data carriers that offer the Gear S2 as of this writing: AT&T, T-Mobile, and Verizon. Finally, the chapter helps you find Gear S2 support on social media networks, including Facebook, Google+, and Twitter, as well as see how to get the latest Gear S2 and Samsung news on the SamMobile website.

Going to the Source

Mr. Spock (both the Nimoy and Quinto versions) would say that the Samsung website is the logical place to start when you want information and support for your Gear S2. You can access the Samsung support website, shown in Figure 13-1, at http://www.samsung.com/us/support/mobile/wearable-tech.

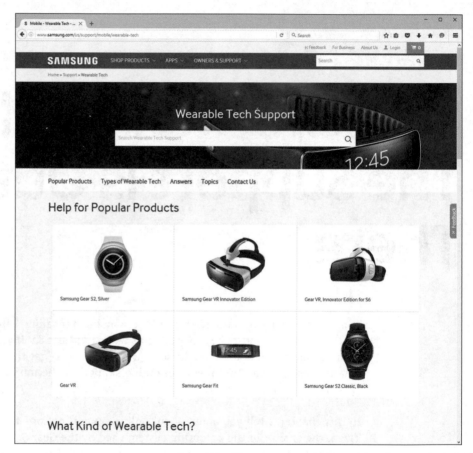

FIGURE 13-1: You can search for topics by typing your terms in the Search box that's in front of the large Samsung Gear Fit near the top of the page.

Source: http://www.samsung.com/us/support/mobile/wearable-tech

The Help for Popular Products section displays two Gear S2 icons. Click Samsung Gear S2, Silver if you have a standard Gear S2. Why Samsung mentions only Silver is one of those mysteries of life, because the help for the Silver Gear S2 is just as valid for the dark gray model. If you have a Gear S2 Classic, click Samsung Gear S2 Classic, Black. You can even click this button if you have the Platinum or Rose Gold Classic models.

If you're a Gear S2 developer, you should bookmark the Samsung Developers website forum at `http://developer.samsung.com/forum/en`. In the forum, tap the Gear check box, shown in Figure 13-2, to read about issues that Gear S2 developers are encountering, answer questions from your fellow developers, and even ask questions of said fellow developers. (They don't bite, and I'm pretty sure they don't bark.)

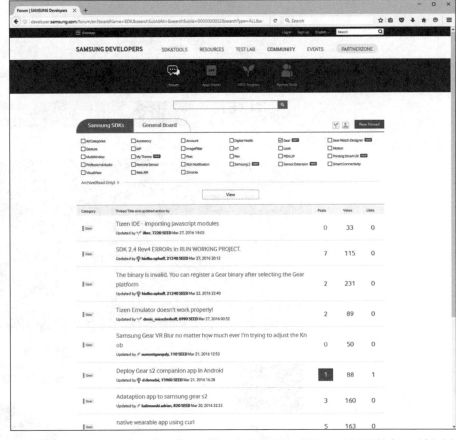

FIGURE 13-2:
Each discussion includes the number of posts in the discussion, the number of views from other forum users, and the number of likes given in the discussion.

Source: `http://developer.samsung.com/forum/en?boardName=SDK&searchSubIdAll=&searchSubold=0000000032&searchType=ALL&`

TIP

If you're thinking about trying your hand at app development on Samsung devices, you should go back to Chapter 11 to read up on development guidelines and the Samsung Gear development website. Then you can visit these websites and dive deeper into developing apps for your Gear S2 — and perhaps find a few more Benjamins in your pocket.

Exploring the Tizen OS

If you want to know about everything Tizen so that you can get the most out of your Gear S2 operating system, going to the Tizen website (`http://www.tizen.org`) would seem logical, but it actually doesn't have a lot of information beyond the basics. A website that offers a lot more news and information about Tizen and devices running that OS is available on the Tizen Experts website at `http://www.tizenexperts.com` (see Figure 13-3).

FIGURE 13-3: The latest news stories appear as multicolored tiles near the top of the Tizen Experts home page.

The Tizen Experts website is a good resource for both users and developers, but if you want to get the Tizen Software Development Kit (SDK), not to mention connect with other developers in the Tizen User Community, check out the Tizen Developers website for wearable devices at `https://developer.tizen.org/tizen/wearable` (see Figure 13-4).

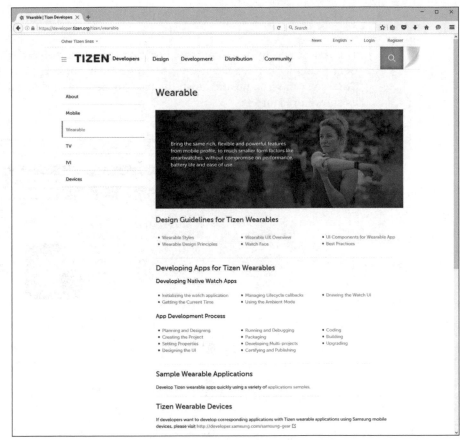

FIGURE 13-4:
The Tizen website has plenty of links to information about design and development.

Source: https://developer.tizen.org/tizen/wearable

This website contains a wide variety of links for designing and developing apps for wearable devices that run the Tizen OS. You can also download a number of app samples that you can learn from. To get access to the samples or participate in the online community, you need to create a new account on the Tizen website and then log in every time you want to view more samples or participate in the forum.

Finding Support from Data Carriers

If you purchased a Gear S2 from a data carrier, you should also look at the carrier's website to get support for its device. This holds especially true if your problem relates to the carrier's network, such as the inability to receive calls. Lest you think I'm playing favorites, the following sections present, in alphabetical order, the three carriers that offer the Gear S2. I visit the three carrier websites on a computer's web browser.

AT&T

The fastest way to find Gear S2 support on the AT&T website is to type **Samsung Gear S2** in the Search box within the orange menu bar at the top of the home page. Then you can scroll up and down the page to view the results on the Results page, as shown in Figure 13-5.

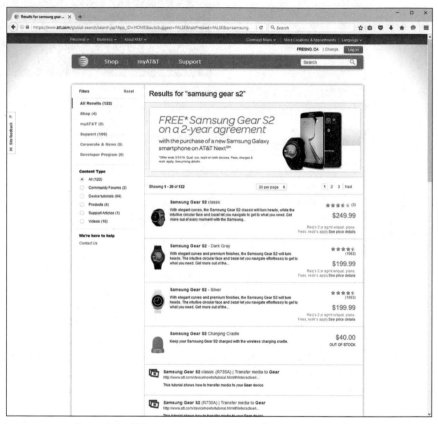

FIGURE 13-5: Scroll down the screen to see support articles in the list.

Source: https://www.att.com/global-search/search.jsp?App-ID=HOME&autoSuggest=
FALSE&tabPressed=FALSE&q=samsung

When you find a document that you want to read, click the document title in the results list. If you don't see the article you want, click the Next link at the bottom of the list to go to the next page of results.

T-Mobile

As with the AT&T site, type **Samsung Gear S2** in the Find box in the menu bar at the top of the screen. The menu bar is plain white but it displays the T-Mobile logo on the left and the My T-Mobile link on the right.

In the Search Results screen that appears (see Figure 13-6), click the Support tab to view a list of all the support documents you can read.

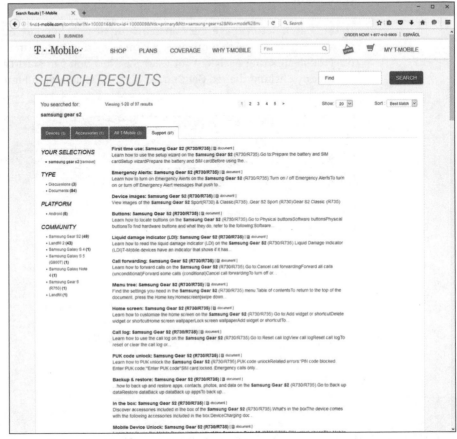

Source: http://find.t-mobile.com/controller?N=1000639&Ntk=primary&Ntt=Samsung+Gear+s2&Ntx=mode%2Bmatchallpartial

FIGURE 13-6:
You know you're in the Support tab because the tab is white with pink text and the other tabs are gray with white text.

Scroll down the screen to view the list of documents and click the document name when you find what you're looking for. If you don't find the article, click the Next button, which is a greater than sign (>), to go to the next page of documents.

Verizon

If you're using the Gear S2 with the Verizon network, Verizon's online troubleshooter might be able to help solve your Gear S2 problems. Start by opening the Verizon website. You can sign into your Verizon account before running the troubleshooter by typing your user ID or mobile number and then clicking the Sign In button.

After you log in, click Support at the top of the page. Within the Support page, look for the Find the Information You Need section, which contains the Search Support box. Type **Samsung Gear S2** and then click the red Search button to the right of the box.

In the Search Results page, click on Samsung Gear S2 Support, and in the Samsung Gear S2 Support page that opens, click on the Troubleshooting tab and then click on Troubleshooting Assistant for Gear S2. Now you can start the online trouble-shooter by clicking the red Get Started button, as shown in Figure 13-7.

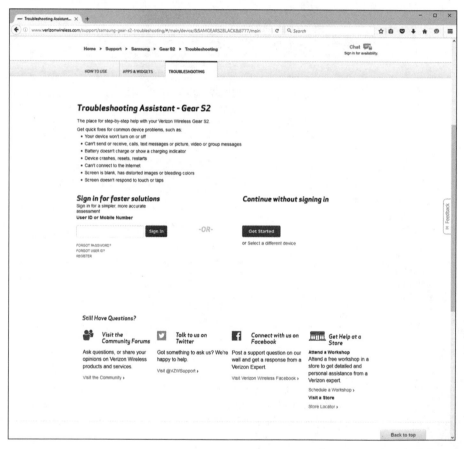

FIGURE 13-7:
Click or tap the
Get Started
button.

Source: www.verizonwireless.com

If you're still having problems after doing some troubleshooting, or want to leave a message for a Verizon representative on Twitter or Facebook, click on the appropriate link in the Still Have Questions? section at the bottom of the page. You can also go to your local Verizon store and talk with a live Verizon employee about your misbehaving gadget.

Visiting Website Communities for Info and Support

You can visit a variety of Gear S2 communities on some of the most popular social networking websites around, including Facebook, Google+, and Twitter. To get the latest news about the Gear S2 and other Samsung technologies, the SamMobile website covers all things Samsung.

Facebook

Facebook has a Gear S2 public group that you can view by typing **Gear S2** in the Search Facebook box (it's in the blue menu bar that appears at the top of your news feed page). As you type, you see the Samsung Gear S2 Group entry in the list. Tap Samsung Gear S2 Group to view the group page, shown in Figure 13-8.

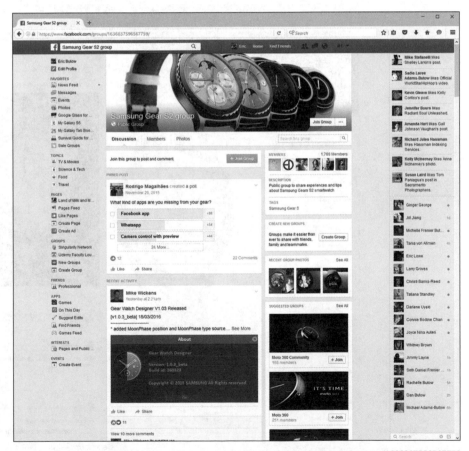

FIGURE 13-8: The Gear S2 Facebook group has more than 1,700 members as of this writing.

Source: www.facebook.com/groups/1636837596567759

Within this group, you can read information by other Gear S2 users. If you want to post messages, reply to existing messages, and do other group-related stuff, you need to join the group by tapping or clicking the green Join Group button on the page.

Google+

Finding the Gear S2 community on Google+ is easy. Just click the Search box in the menu bar (or tap the Search button within the mobile Google+ website), type **Samsung Gear S2** in the box, and then click or tap Samsung Gear S & Gear S2 in the list that appears below the Search box.

Now all you have to do to follow the Samsung Gear S & Gear S2 community is click or tap the white Follow button on the screen. Then you can not only read the latest posts about the Gear family of watches, as shown in Figure 13-9, but also write replies to existing posts and write your own posts.

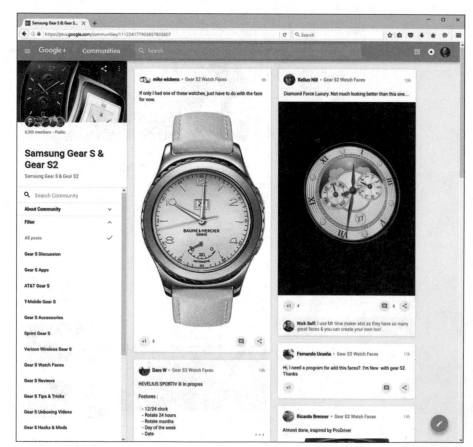

FIGURE 13-9: You can include pictures within your posts, including some of your latest watch faces.

Source: https://plus.google.com/communities/

SamMobile

You can keep track of what's happening with the Gear S2 and other products in the Samsung ecosphere by visiting the SamMobile website at `http://www.sammobile.com`, shown in Figure 13-10.

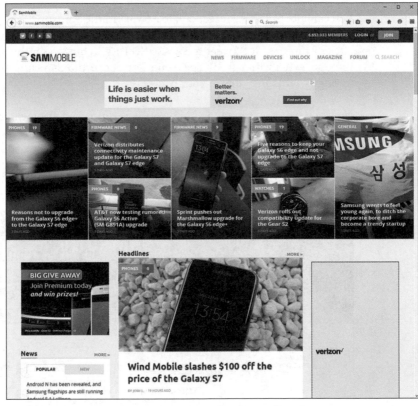

Source: www.sammobile.com

FIGURE 13-10: Read one of the most recent news stories by tapping a large story tile at the top of the page.

This website has breaking news often before any other Samsung website does. SamMobile also includes news about the latest firmware (that is, system software) for Samsung devices, instructional videos, and an online forum in which to chat with other users. If you want to get the most from the SamMobile site, such as the ability to participate in the forum, you need to create a SamMobile account and then log into your account whenever you visit the site.

Twitter

Though no Gear S2 account exists on Twitter, you can follow the Samsung Developers Twitter account if you want to develop apps for fun and profit. Just type

Samsung dev in the Search Twitter box within the menu bar that appears at the top of your Twitter feed page. Now click Samsung Developers in the results list that appears below the Search Twitter box.

Now you can follow the Samsung Developers Twitter feed by tapping Follow on the page shown in Figure 13-11.

You can like, retweet, or respond to a tweet in the Samsung Developers feed as you would with any other tweet. If you want to tweet to the Samsung Developers feed, click or tap the blue Tweet to SAMSUNG DEVEL button on the page. When you're in your own Twitter feed page, send a tweet to the Samsung Developers feed by typing **@samsung_dev** in your tweet.

Now you can get communicating. You'll be surprised at how many fellow Gear S2 users are interested in hearing about what you're up to.

FIGURE 13-11: The Follow button appears at the right side of the Twitter feed page just below the huge Samsung Developer Conference logo in this example.

Source: https://twitter.com/samsung_dev

5
The Part of Tens

IN THIS PART . . .

Learning how to use the Status Panel to check vital information and change the screen brightness level

Placing your Gear S2 into Do Not Disturb mode

Accessing apps from the Status Panel and using the bezel

Changing and selecting new widgets

Selecting new watch faces from the Galaxy Apps store

Designing your own watch faces

Discovering ten apps for the Gear S2 that will make your daily life with the Gear S2 more productive, satisfying, and fun

Chapter 14

Ten Ways to Use Your Gear S2 More Efficiently

H aving a smartwatch that can play music, respond to your commands, measure your heart rate, and lots more can make some aspects of your life more efficient. But you can use it more efficiently yet by knowing some tricks that you can take advantage of to make your life easier, and that's what this chapter is for. These are things like checking information and accessing functions quickly, replacing the default app icons in the widget with new ones, using the bezel to access apps in the Apps screen, and changing watch faces quickly from the watch screen.

Using Shortcuts on the Status Panel

When you're in the watch screen, you can access a hidden method to find out the current status of your connection and battery level, change the screen brightness, listen to your music, and tell your Gear S2 not to disturb you. Here's the secret sauce: Just hold your finger at the top of the screen and then swipe down to open the Status Panel.

Checking the connection and battery level

When you open the Status Panel, you see the battery icon at the top of the screen and the battery strength percentage just below the icon. If the Bluetooth feature is on, you see a Bluetooth icon to the right of the battery icon, as shown at the top of Figure 14-1.

If you aren't connected to your smartphone when you open the Status Panel, you see the word Standalone on the screen.

FIGURE 14-1:
The Status level tells you that you're connected to your smartphone via Bluetooth.

Turning on Do Not Disturb

When you're using your Gear S2 to do something important, having notifications keep buzzing and showing up on your Gear S2 screen gets old quickly. Fortunately, you can turn off notifications by tapping the Do Not Disturb icon at the bottom of the screen (refer to Figure 14-1).

When the Do Not Disturb screen appears (see Figure 14-2), tap the Confirm icon on the right side of the screen to turn on Do Not Disturb. If you change your mind, tap the Cancel icon on the left side of the screen.

FIGURE 14-2:
The Confirm icon has a check mark in it.

The watch screen reappears, and the Do Not Disturb icon displays at the top of the screen in front of the 12 o'clock marker on the watch face (see Figure 14-3).

As long as you see the Do Not Disturb icon, you won't see or hear any notifications, but you will see and hear alarms if you have set one or more alarms in the Alarm app.

When you decide that it's time to receive notifications again, open the Status Panel. When the Do Not Disturb icon shows a green bar, the feature is on (see Figure 14-4). Tap the Do Not Disturb icon to turn the feature off.

FIGURE 14-3:
The Do Not Disturb icon is a white minus sign inside a circle.

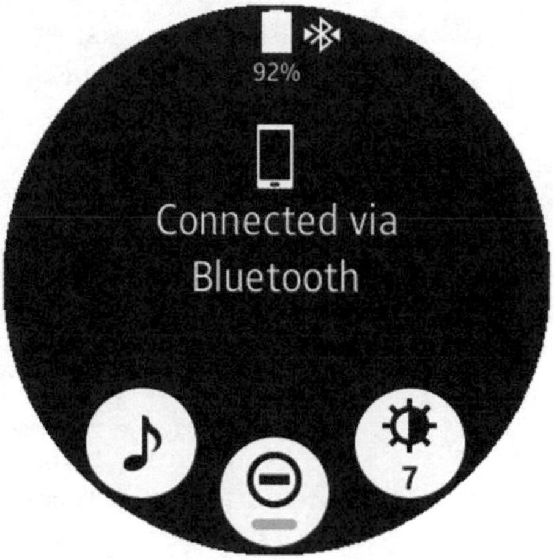

FIGURE 14-4:
The green bar appears within the Do Not Disturb icon.

The watch screen appears again, and the Do Not Disturb icon no longer appears at the top of the screen.

Adjusting the brightness level

If your screen brightness is hurting your eyes because it's too bright or too dark and you want to change the brightness level fast, open the Status Panel and then tap the Brightness icon (see Figure 14-5). The icon includes the current brightness level as a number between 1 and 10, and the default number is 7.

FIGURE 14-5:
The Brightness icon appears at the 5 o'clock position on the screen.

Change the brightness level by rotating the bezel to the left and right. As you move the bezel, the screen brightens or dims accordingly and the number changes as well, showing you the brightness level corresponding to the number. The blue line around the perimeter of the screen shown in Figure 14-6 also grows or shrinks, respectively, when you increase or decrease the brightness.

When you finish setting the brightness, press the Back button to return to the watch screen.

FIGURE 14-6:
The current brightness level number appears at the top of the screen.

Accessing the Music Player fast

If you're ready to dance or run or walk to the music stored on your Gear S2 or your smartphone, you don't have to go through the hassle of swiping the screen from right to left to find the Music Player widget. Instead, open the Status Panel and then tap the Music Player button (see Figure 14-7).

Now you can start playing and managing your music in the Music Player app (see Figure 14-8). If you want to learn more about using the Music Player app, check out Chapter 7.

FIGURE 14-7:
The Music Player button appears at the 7 o'clock position on the screen.

FIGURE 14-8:
Start playing the song by tapping the Play icon in the center of the screen.

Changing the App Shortcuts Widget Apps

The App Shortcuts widget allows you to tap one of four app icons to access apps that you use most often. The default apps that you can access in the widget are Apps, Buddy, Settings, and S Voice. However, you can change one or all four of these apps to get quicker access to the apps you use the most.

One minor detail to deal with is the fact that the App Shortcuts widget is not installed on your Gear S2 by default. You can add it easily, though, and after which you can start replacing apps within the widget.

To add the App Shortcuts widget in the watch screen, swipe from right to left on the screen repeatedly (or rotate the bezel to the right) until you see the Add Widget screen, shown in Figure 14-9. Tap the Add Widget icon.

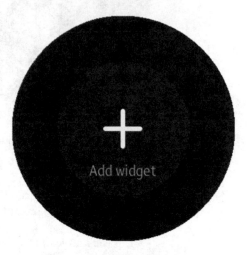

Swipe from right to left once, or rotate the bezel to the right until you feel a click. The App Shortcuts widget image appears in the center of the screen (see Figure 14-10). Tap the widget image to add the widget to your Gear S2.

FIGURE 14-9:
You can't miss the Add widget icon on the screen.

You can use the App Shortcuts widget when it appears on the screen, but to edit the widget, you need to tap and hold the center of the screen (in the blank spot between all four icons) for a couple of seconds until you feel the Gear S2 vibrate. Then the Edit screen appears, as shown in Figure 14-11.

Start making changes by tapping the Edit icon. Each of the four icons includes a Delete icon in the upper-right area, as shown in Figure 14-12.

FIGURE 14-10:
The widget title appears at the bottom of the screen.

FIGURE 14-11:
The Edit icon appears at the bottom of the Edit screen.

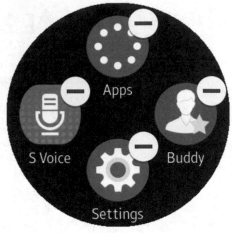

FIGURE 14-12:
The Delete icons are red minus signs inside white circles.

To remove an app, tap the Delete icon in the upper-right corner of the app icon. The icon disappears and an Add icon appears (see Figure 14-13).

Tap the Add icon to view the list of apps you can add. The currently selected app icon and name appear in the center of the screen, as shown in Figure 14-14. Swipe right and left on the screen, or rotate the bezel right and left, to scroll through the list of the apps you can add.

FIGURE 14-13:
The Add icon is a plus sign inside a circle.

FIGURE 14-14:
The currently selected icon appears in the center of the screen.

Tap the app's icon to add it to the App Shortcuts widget. The current four icons appear in the App Shortcuts screen. Each of the icons includes a Delete icon, as shown in Figure 14-15, in case you want to replace any of them.

Press the Back button to return to the Edit screen, and press the Back button again to return to the App Shortcuts widget so that you can tap any of your current app icons.

FIGURE 14-15:
The app you just added appears at the 3 o'clock position on the screen.

Using the Bezel to Access Apps

When you open the Apps screen, you can rotate the bezel left and right to highlight an app icon on the screen, enabling you to open it as well as move back and forth between Apps screen pages. (The side benefit is that moving the bezel makes you look like a suave secret agent.)

Using the bezel to open an app

When you move the bezel to the right and left, the white selection dot appears next to the icon you selected (see Figure 14-16). When the selection dot appears next to the icon, the icon gets a little larger and you can see the name of the app in the middle of the screen. You can still tap the icon to open the app, but you can also tap the name of the selected app to open it.

FIGURE 14-16:
The Settings app icon has the selection dot next to it, and the app name appears in the center of the screen.

Moving between app screen pages

As you move the bezel to the right, the selection dot will eventually rest next to the Next Page icon at the 11 o'clock position on the screen. You can view the next page in one of two ways: by tapping the center of the screen or rotating the bezel to the right. Then you see the next page, as shown in Figure 14-17.

The first icon selected in the second Apps screen page is Previous Page. You can return to the first page by either tapping the center of the screen or by moving the bezel to the left. Your selection dot will then rest on the last app icon on the first page, which is the Weather app.

Now keep moving the bezel to the right until you see the selection dot appear next to the Next Page icon, as shown in Figure 14-18.

FIGURE 14-17:
The Previous Page icon is at the 1 o'clock position on the screen.

FIGURE 14-18:
The Next Page icon is at the 11 o'clock position on the screen.

Now move the bezel to the right to go forward to the third page and select from one of the icons on that page. If you want to return to the first page of apps, you have to use the bezel or just swipe the screen twice from left to right.

Quickly Accessing Watch Info and Changing Watch Faces

One of the most amazing features of the Gear S2 is the ability to change your watch face to one that reflects your coolness, mood, or current taste. I tell you how to change watch faces in Chapter 3, but there are faster ways to access watch information and change the watch face from the watch screen itself. What's more, you can download Samsung's Gear Watch Designer for free so that you can design your own watch face.

Accessing battery and steps information

If you're looking at a watch face that has battery and steps information on it, such as the Modern Utility face that's the standard watch face on the Gear S2 Classic, you can tap the Battery and Steps icons on the face to get battery and steps information, as shown in Figure 14-19.

When you tap the Battery icon, you see the battery level percentage on the screen (see Figure 14-20) as well as a green line around the perimeter of the screen that gets shorter as your Gear S2 battery strength drops.

FIGURE 14-19:
You can tap the Steps icon on the watch face even if one of the hands partially blocks the icon.

FIGURE 14-20:
The battery level percentage appears in the center of the screen.

When you tap the Steps icon in the watch face, you open the Steps widget, which tells you how many steps you've taken and how your steps today compare with the number of steps you took each day during the past week.

Changing watch faces

Here's a fast way to open the watch faces screen and select a new watch face: Tap and hold your finger on the center of the watch screen for three seconds until you feel the Gear S2 vibrate. The Modern Utility face appears in the watch faces screen (see Figure 14-21), enabling you to stylize that face or select a new face.

Creating your own watch face with Gear Watch Designer

FIGURE 14-21:
The Modern Utility face appears on the watch faces screen.

If you're dissatisfied with the selection of watch faces both on your Gear S2 and on the Galaxy Apps app, you can do something about it: Create one yourself. Samsung has made its Gear Watch Designer available to download for free. Maybe you can even earn some money by uploading and selling your creations on the Galaxy Apps store.

You can get more information and download Gear Watch Designer on the Samsung Developers website at http://developer.samsung.com/gear/design/watch-designer. Within the Gear Watch Designer web page (see Figure 14-22), Samsung reminds you that the app is in beta (at least as of this writing), so using the app won't be all happy white clouds.

If you want to try the Gear Watch Designer to see how it works for you, download the app for either Windows or the Mac OS by clicking the buttons that appear above the video tutorial on the page. If you want to see a static image of the app, scroll down the page to view the image shown in Figure 14-23.

Samsung designed the Gear Watch Designer interface to be familiar to anyone who has used graphic apps such as Adobe Photoshop. Even if you're not much into graphics and you're a bit intimidated by what's in the static image of the app, Samsung makes it easy for beginners to get up to speed, too.

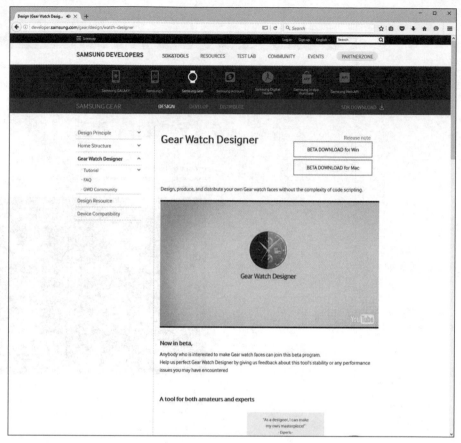

FIGURE 14-22:
A brief video tutorial starts playing when you open the Gear Watch Designer web page.

Source: www.samsung.com/gear/design/watch-designer

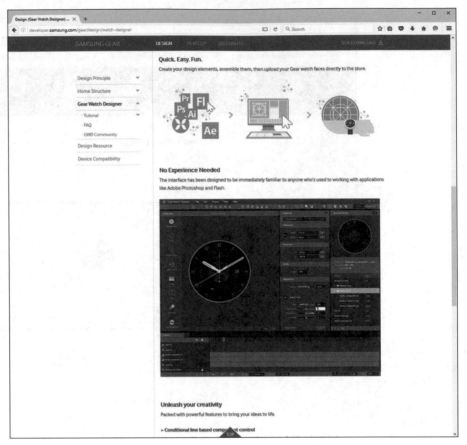

FIGURE 14-23:
The screen-
shot of the
Gear Watch
Designer
app gives
you a sense
of how to
design a new
watch face.

Source: developer.samsung.com/gear/design/watch-designer

Chapter 15

Ten Cool (and Free!) Gear S2 Apps

P lenty of apps are available for the Gear S2, with hundreds of apps available as of this writing. However, you may be disappointed to learn that Samsung considers watch faces to be apps, and finding actual apps in the Google Apps store may be hard. You can find more than a few nonwatch face apps within the 300 free apps listed in the Galaxy Apps store as of this writing, though, so you can download apps and try them without being out a few bucks. For this chapter, I've picked ten free apps that run the gamut from useful to fun. You can use these apps to make your Gear S2 serve as calculator, a handy flashlight, and a walkie-talkie — and even for eBay shopping, locating your car in a parking lot, finding a ride, and playing games.

REMEMBER

To see how to find, download, and install an app, as well as find your newly installed app in the Apps screen, check out Chapter 10.

Discovering Useful Utilities

The Gear S2 already comes with a number of utility apps and widgets preinstalled, such as the Timer app. This section tells you about two other utilities you should consider installing on your Gear S2 after you're comfortable using the device.

Calculator

I cover how to download and install the Calculator app in Chapter 10. Calculator is a great utility to have when you need to make a quick calculation. (Not every restaurant leaves the suggested tip amounts on its receipts.) After you install the app, you just tap the calculator keys to perform an operation (see Figure 15-1).

You can perform only simple arithmetic calculations: addition, subtraction, multiplication, and division. In the upper third of the screen, along with the operation you're performing, you also see the result after you tap the green equal key at the bottom of the screen.

FIGURE 15-1:
The operation in this example is 35 x 0.18 to calculate an 18 percent tip.

FlashLight S2

Smartphones have flashlight apps that let you use your smartphone flash as a flashlight. You'll be pleasantly surprised to know that you can use your Gear S2 screen as a flashlight as well with FlashLight S2.

FlashLight S2 has three functions:

>> **Flashlight:** The screen acts as a flashlight with a light color you select. Then you can rotate your arm so the screen points to whatever you want to illuminate. The light on your screen can be seen from about a mile away (or a little over 1.5 kilometers away, for our friends outside the U.S.).

>> **Strobe light:** Turn your Gear S2 into a strobe light to get someone's attention. You can change the light color as well as the speed of the flashes.

>> **SOS:** This light flashes SOS in Morse code, so anyone who sees it (such as from a law enforcement agency) and knows the SOS pattern will know that you're calling for help.

After you install and start FlashLight S2, tap the screen or rotate the bezel to the right to open the menu, shown in Figure 15-2. By default, the entire screen is bright white when you tap the large white circle in the center of the screen. Rotate the bezel to the left to change the color of the flashlight.

As you rotate the bezel, the selected color, which is the large circle in the center of the screen, changes. The yellow selection triangle also moves next to the color swatch that appears in the perimeter of the screen. Tap the selected color circle to show the entire color on the screen so that you can use the screen as a flashlight. Return to the menu by tapping the screen.

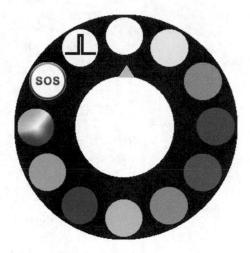

FIGURE 15-2:
The yellow selection triangle appears below the white color swatch at the 12 o'clock position on the screen.

At the 9 o'clock position on the screen, you see a multicolored swatch. When you move the bezel to point the select triangle to this swatch, the selected color circle in the middle of the screen quickly switches among colors.

When you move the select triangle to the 10 o'clock position on the screen, the selected color circle flashes in the SOS pattern. Tap the circle to start flashing the SOS pattern.

At the 11 o'clock position on the screen, you see the strobe light icon. When you move the select triangle to the strobe light icon, the selected color circle begins flashing so that you can see how fast the strobe light flashes. Tap the selected color circle to run the strobe light on the entire screen. Then you can rotate the bezel to change the speed of the strobe flashes. Tapping the middle of the screen changes the strobe light color or turns off the strobe light.

Sending and Receiving Messages

You can already send and receive messages on your Gear S2 using preinstalled apps such as Email and Messaging. But apps for keeping you up-to-date with your social media feeds are still slow in coming as of this writing. If you use Twitter, you're in luck, albeit in a limited way: You can check the latest Twitter trends and read tweets in those trend categories by using the Trends for Gear app.

What's more, if you have the 3G version of the Gear S2 (that's the Standard or black Classic models), you can use the Voxer app as your own personal walkie-talkie. That is, you can speak into your Gear S2 and send your voice message to another Gear S2-with-3G user. That person can then use Voxer to talk back to you. It's like having your own little spy network accessible from your wrist.

Trends for Gear

If you're even a casual Twitter user, you've probably noticed the Trends section on the Twitter website that shows what topics are generating the most tweets from fellow Twitter users (or is that Twitterers?) in your area. The Trends for Gear app for your Gear S2 shows the top five trends in the area that's already set in your Twitter account. You can tap the trend name and then view a list of tweets in that category.

FIGURE 15-3:
Your selected trend in the list.

After you install Trends for Gear, the app asks you to use your location to show your local content. Tap the blue Confirm icon at the bottom of the screen to continue. Now you see the Trends screen, and you can rotate the bezel to the right to view the five most popular trends. The selected trend appears in white text within a blue box in the center of the screen shown, as shown in Figure 15-3.

Tap the trend name and then rotate your bezel to the right to view the top five tweets within the trend (see Figure 15-4). If you want to read the story on the website associated with the tweet on your smartphone, tap the tweet text. Your smartphone asks you what browser app you want to

FIGURE 15-4:
A tweet may also include a photo too small to figure out what it is.

open to view the website (or open the browser app if you've selected one to use all the time) so that you can read the article on your smartphone screen.

Voxer

Voxer has realized the dreams of every Dick Tracy fan (or at least compelled you to find out who he is) by bringing the two-way wrist radio to life — that is, if you purchased a 3G version of your Gear S2 so that you can use your phone carrier's data network to send and receive Voxer audio messages with one or more people in your contact list (who have a Gear S2 with 3G and Voxer, of course). You can even send and view photos as well as preview text messages.

After you install Voxer on your Gear S2, you need to install Voxer with either your Android smartphone or your iPhone. After you start Voxer on your phone, you need to create a new account by typing your account password into your phone. Then you need to watch for notice of an email message sent by Voxer that asks you to verify your email address.

After your Voxer account is set up, open the Voxer app on the Gear S2. A list of your contacts who also use Voxer appears in the contact list. Rotate the bezel until your selected contact appears in the center of the screen. (The selected contact also has larger, white text, so you can't miss it.) Tap the contact name and then tap and hold the orange walkie-talkie icon to begin communicating (see Figure 15-5). When the icon turns green, you can start talking. As you talk, a timer on the screen shows you how long you've been talking.

FIGURE 15-5:
The walkie-talkie icon takes up the bottom half of the screen.

When you're finished talking, release your finger from the screen. Voxer immediately sends the message to the other person. If that other person uses Voxer on his or her smartphone, Gear S2, or both, the person will receive your voice message.

However, because Voxer connects to other devices using the device's phone number, you won't receive messages sent by another Voxer user to your Gear S2 unless you have a 3G model bestowed upon you by your favorite (or tolerated) phone carrier.

Shopping on Your Gear S2

If you have an eBay account, you can check on items you're bidding on and see who's bidding on items you're selling just by looking at the Gear S2. If you're at a store and you want to use a coupon for something you want to buy without having to carry a paper coupon in your hand, you can use the FidMe app on your Gear S2.

eBay for Gear

The eBay for Gear app is one of those apps that require the installation of a companion app on your smartphone. What's more, that smartphone needs to be an Android smartphone. If you're undaunted at this point, here's how to install eBay for your Gear S2:

1. **In the watch screen on the Gear S2, press the Home button.**

   The Apps screen opens.

2. **Swipe from right to left on the screen until you see the third page in the Apps screen.**

   The Music Player app icon is selected on the screen by default.

3. **Tap the Get More Apps icon.**

   The icon appears at the 11 o'clock position on the screen.

4. **In the Galaxy Apps screen on your smartphone, tap Top Free.**

   The Top Free link appears in the dark-gray section bar above the list of featured Gear apps.

5. **Swipe upward in the screen until you see eBay for Gear; then tap eBay for Gear in the list.**

   The Details screen opens and shows information about the eBay for Gear app.

6. **Tap the blue Install button on the screen.**

   After the Galaxy Apps app installs the eBay for Gear app on your Gear S2, the eBay for Gear window appears on the smartphone screen.

7. **Tap OK.**

   The Google Play Store window open and displays the eBay for Gear Companion app details page.

8. **Tap Install.**

   The eBay for Gear Companion permissions window appears.

9. **Tap Accept.**

After the Google Play Store app installs the eBay for Gear Companion app, the eBay for Gear Companion app details screen appears again.

10. **Tap Open.**

The introductory eBay for Gear screen appears.

11. **Tap the blue Agree & Continue button.**

The blue Sign In button appears at the bottom of the screen.

12. **Tap Sign In.**

The login screen appears.

13. **Type your eBay user ID and password.**

Now you can swipe up and down the eBay for Gear Companion app screen, shown in Figure 15-6, to view the types of notifications you want to see in the eBay app screen on your Gear S2.

If you don't want to view notifications in a certain category, such as having been outbid on an item, tap the blue selected check box next to the notification type name shown in Figure 15-6. Tapping the check box deselects this notification.

Now turn your attention to the Gear S2, press the Home button, and then navigate to the Apps screen page that contains the eBay icon. After you tap the eBay icon, the eBay screen appears and tells you that you have no notifications (see Figure 15-7).

Tap the Settings icon on the right side of the screen to view the Download the eBay App icon within the Settings screen. When you tap this icon, the Google Play Store opens on your smartphone and opens the eBay app details screen so that you can download the full eBay app to your smartphone.

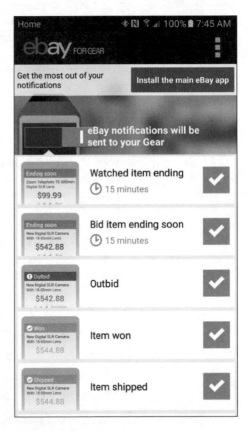

FIGURE 15-6:
Selected notification types have a blue box with a white check mark that appears to the right of the type name.

When you open the eBay app on your Gear S2, you'll still be in the Settings screen, but you can return to the Notifications screen by tapping the Back button on the left side of the screen.

I say this at the risk of sounding like an Emergency Alert System test, but if you had received an actual notification, you would see a list of notifications on the screen with the most recent notification on the top of the screen. Tap a notification to read it and perhaps perform an action depending on the type of notification. For example, if the notification says you've been outbid on an item, you'll be asked to increase your bid by tapping the Increase Bid icon at the bottom of the screen.

FIGURE 15-7:
If no activity has occurred on your item, you see No Activity in the center of the screen.

FidMe

FidMe uses both an app on your Gear S2 and an app on your smartphone to gather all your loyalty card, coupon, and deal information so that you can quickly check them with just a press and a few taps on your Gear S2. Unlike the eBay app, which is available only for Android, the FidMe app runs on both iPhone and Android smartphones.

Because I use an Android smartphone with my Gear S2 throughout this book, this example shows you how to install FidMe with an Android smartphone. So here's how to install FidMe:

1. **In the watch screen on the Gear S2, press the Home button.**

    The Apps screen opens.

2. **Swipe from right to left on the screen until you see the third page in the Apps screen.**

    The Music Player app icon is selected on the screen by default.

3. **Tap the Get More Apps icon.**

    The icon appears at the 11 o'clock position on the screen.

4. **In the Galaxy Apps screen on your smartphone, tap Top Free.**

    The Top Free link appears in the dark-gray section bar above the list of featured Gear apps.

5. **Swipe upward in the screen until you see FidMe and then tap FidMe in the list.**

The Details screen opens and shows information about the FidMe app.

6. **Tap the blue Install icon on the screen.**

After the Galaxy Apps app installs the FidMe app on your Gear S2, the FidMe window appears on the smartphone screen.

7. **Tap OK.**

The Google Play Store window open and displays the FidMe Loyalty Cards & Coupons app details page.

8. **Tap Install.**

The FidMe Loyalty Cards & Coupons permissions window appears.

9. **Tap Accept.**

After the Google Play Store app installs the eBay for Gear Companion app, the eBay for Gear Companion app details screen appears again.

10. **Tap Open.**

The FidMe app screen appears on your smartphone, and you can swipe back and forth to view basic information about FidMe in the introduction window.

11. **Tap the Close icon in the upper-right corner of the introduction window.**

The Welcome to FidMe screen appears so that you can sign into your FidMe account or create a new account by tapping the Account Sign Up icon.

After you log in, you can add one or more reward cards on the FidMe smartphone app. Once you've entered a card, you may want to wait a few minutes for the FidMe smartphone app to sync with the FidMe Gear S2 app. Next, press the Home button on the Gear S2, navigate to the page in the Apps screen that contains the FidMe icon, and then tap the FidMe icon. You see your newly added card name on the screen (see Figure 15-8).

Now tap the card name to show the barcode of your card on the screen. If the cashier or server has a barcode reader, all you have to do is have the

FIGURE 15-8:
Yummm!

cashier scan the barcode on your Gear S2 screen so you can get the reward you deserve.

Finding Your Ride

When you're in a city and you don't have a ride, one option you have to get around is to catch a ride with an Uber driver. As of this writing, Uber is the only car-for-hire company that has an app for the Gear S2. Or, if you have your own car but you can't remember where you parked it, there's an app for that, too, as described in this section.

Uber

When you download the Uber app for the Gear S2 from the Galaxy Apps app, you see that the Phone App Also check box is selected by default (see Figure 15-9). Keep this check box selected because you must also install the Uber Companion app for your smartphone.

Unfortunately, I live in a small town, so I can't use Uber, but the Details screen shown in Figure 15-9 includes several screenshots of the app, with information about how long you have to wait for your ride to get to your location. This information shows you what you can expect when you use your Gear S2 as an uber Uber user.

Find My Car

The story of being unable to find your car in a large parking lot is ingrained into (at least) modern American culture. Now with your Gear S2, you don't have to worry about finding your car because you can install Samsung's Find My Car app on your smartwatch.

FIGURE 15-9:
The Phone App Also check box appears under the rating stars.

After you install the app and start it on your Gear S2, the introductory screen appears, telling you that you need to use location-based services to continue using the app. Tap the Confirm icon on the right side of the screen to open the Welcome screen and read information about how the app uses your information. Tap the Confirm icon at the right side of the screen to open the New Parking screen.

In the New Parking screen, tap the New Parking icon in the center of the screen to see a map that has your current location as a green pin icon. You need to be next to your car so that you can see your current location, and you can rotate the bezel to the right to zoom in on the map and rotate the bezel to the right to zoom out on the map.

Tap the green pin icon in the map to open the Parking Memo recording app so that you can record an audio reminder of where you are. You can record up to 30 seconds of audio. Start recording by tapping the Record icon, shown in Figure 15-10.

Now you can start talking to your Gear S2. When you're done, tap the orange Stop icon in the middle of the screen. The play screen appears (see Figure 15-11). Now you can go do what you planned to do and when you come back out to try to find out where you parked, tap the Play icon.

FIGURE 15-10:
The Record icon is a large white circle with a small red circle inside it.

FIGURE 15-11:
The orange Play icon appears in the center of the screen.

If you want to go back to the map view after you listen to your audio instructions, press the Back button and you'll see your current location.

Gaming on Your Wrist

Games aren't just for wasting your time on smartphones anymore. The Gear S2 makes it easy for you to play games even on the small Gear S2 screen so that you can take a well-deserved break and give your brain some exercise. Two popular games as of this writing are Crush Words Lite and Snake.

Crush Words Lite

Crush Words Lite shows you nine letter tiles in a 3-x-3 grid. The letters in the grid make up two related words, and you have to try to figure out what the two words are.

After you download and install Crush Words Lite, you can start by tapping Play in the Crush Words introductory screen. Then you see the puzzle shown in Figure 15-12.

Tap, hold, and drag your finger vertically or horizontally over the letter tiles that you think make up one of the words. You have to move your finger over each letter of the word in order. When you get to the last letter of the word, release your finger.

If you select the right word, the letters disappear and you see only the remaining letters of the second word. Tap, hold, and drag your finger over the letters in the second word.

FIGURE 15-12:
The first word in the first puzzle is BOY.

Tap the screen twice to get three hints about the puzzle in the Hints screen. Tap the Resume icon in the Hints screen to return to the puzzle. You can solve seven puzzles, which the game calls levels. When you've solved all seven puzzles, you get invited to pay for the full version of Crush Words with 80 levels and 10 hints for $1.50.

Snake Classic S2

The classic game Snake is a natural fit for the Gear S2, and you can download Snake Classic S2 from the Galaxy Apps store for free. After you install Snake Classic S2 and launch the app on the Gear S2, you see the Snake Classic opening screen.

The first time you play the game, you see an instruction screen that tells you to rotate your bezel left and right to control the direction of the snake. The next time you play Snake Classic S2, you don't see this instruction screen.

The snake moves automatically, but you can change the direction of the snake to try to touch the snake food, which is just a stationary black dot (see Figure 15-13). When your snake eats the food, the size of the snake grows and the location of the dot moves to another location on the screen.

Now you can try to move your snake to eat more food and grow your snake as long as you can. If the snake touches itself or the perimeter of the screen, the game ends.

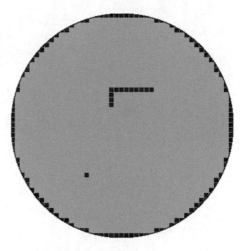

FIGURE 15-13:
Snakes like grass, so keep your snake within the green play area.

When the game is over, you see the number of points you received for eating the snake food in the Game Over screen. Return to the opening screen by tapping the blue Confirm icon at the bottom of the screen. Then you can tap on the opening screen to play a new game.

Index

Notes

Notes

About the Author

Eric Butow began writing books in 2000 when he wrote *Master Visually Windows 2000 Server* (IDG). Since then, Eric has authored or coauthored 29 other books, including *Google Glass For Dummies* (Wiley). Eric, who lives in Jackson, California, holds a master's degree in communication from California State University, Fresno, and is the owner of Butow Communications Group (BCG), an online marketing ROI improvement firm. Go to his website at `http://butow.net` and find him on LinkedIn at `http://linkedin.com/in/ebutow`.

Dedication

To my mother, who never stops working.

Author's Acknowledgments

My thanks as always to my family and friends. I also want to thank my awesome literary agent, Carole Jelen, as well as my wonderful editors, Susan Christophersen and Katie Mohr.

Publisher's Acknowledgments

Executive Editor: Katie Mohr

Project Manager and Copy Editor:
Susan Christophersen

Sr. Editorial Assistant: Cherie Case

Production Editor: Siddique Shaik

Cover Image: Abstract background: tashechka/
Shutterstock; Samsung Gear S2: Butow
Communications Group

& Mac

r Dummies,
ition
118-72306-7

e For Dummies,
ition
118-69083-3

All-in-One
ummies, 4th Edition
118-82210-4

Mavericks
ummies
118-69188-5

ing & Social Media

ook For Dummies,
ition
118-63312-0

Media Engagement
ummies
118-53019-1

Press For Dummies,
ition
118-79161-5

ess

Investing
ummies, 4th Edition
118-37678-2

ing For Dummies,
ition
470-90545-6

**Personal Finance
For Dummies, 7th Edition**
978-1-118-11785-9

**QuickBooks 2014
For Dummies**
978-1-118-72005-9

**Small Business Marketing
Kit For Dummies,
3rd Edition**
978-1-118-31183-7

Careers

Job Interviews
For Dummies, 4th Edition
978-1-118-11290-8

Job Searching with Social
Media For Dummies,
2nd Edition
978-1-118-67856-5

Personal Branding
For Dummies
978-1-118-11792-7

Resumes For Dummies,
6th Edition
978-0-470-87361-8

Starting an Etsy Business
For Dummies, 2nd Edition
978-1-118-59024-9

Diet & Nutrition

Belly Fat Diet For Dummies
978-1-118-34585-6

Mediterranean Diet
For Dummies
978-1-118-71525-3

Nutrition For Dummies,
5th Edition
978-0-470-93231-5

Digital Photography

Digital SLR Photography
All-in-One For Dummies,
2nd Edition
978-1-118-59082-9

Digital SLR Video &
Filmmaking For Dummies
978-1-118-36598-4

Photoshop Elements 12
For Dummies
978-1-118-72714-0

Gardening

Herb Gardening
For Dummies, 2nd Edition
978-0-470-61778-6

Gardening with Free-Range
Chickens For Dummies
978-1-118-54754-0

Health

Boosting Your Immunity
For Dummies
978-1-118-40200-9

Diabetes For Dummies,
4th Edition
978-1-118-29447-5

Living Paleo For Dummies
978-1-118-29405-5

Big Data

Big Data For Dummies
978-1-118-50422-2

Data Visualization
For Dummies
978-1-118-50289-1

Hadoop For Dummies
978-1-118-60755-8

Language &
Foreign Language

500 Spanish Verbs
For Dummies
978-1-118-02382-2

English Grammar
For Dummies, 2nd Edition
978-0-470-54664-2

French All-in-One
For Dummies
978-1-118-22815-9

German Essentials
For Dummies
978-1-118-18422-6

Italian For Dummies,
2nd Edition
978-1-118-00465-4

Available in print and e-book formats.

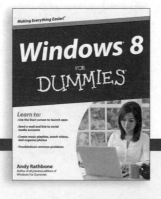

Available wherever books are sold. **For more information or to order direct visit www.dummies.com**

Math & Science

Algebra I For Dummies,
2nd Edition
978-0-470-55964-2

Anatomy and Physiology
For Dummies, 2nd Edition
978-0-470-92326-9

Astronomy For Dummies,
3rd Edition
978-1-118-37697-3

Biology For Dummies,
2nd Edition
978-0-470-59875-7

Chemistry For Dummies,
2nd Edition
978-1-118-00730-3

1001 Algebra II Practice
Problems For Dummies
978-1-118-44662-1

Microsoft Office

Excel 2013 For Dummies
978-1-118-51012-4

Office 2013 All-in-One
For Dummies
978-1-118-51636-2

PowerPoint 2013
For Dummies
978-1-118-50253-2

Word 2013 For Dummies
978-1-118-49123-2

Music

Blues Harmonica
For Dummies
978-1-118-25269-7

Guitar For Dummies,
3rd Edition
978-1-118-11554-1

iPod & iTunes
For Dummies, 10th Edition
978-1-118-50864-0

Programming

Beginning Programming
with C For Dummies
978-1-118-73763-7

Excel VBA Programming
For Dummies, 3rd Edition
978-1-118-49037-2

Java For Dummies,
6th Edition
978-1-118-40780-6

Religion & Inspiration

The Bible For Dummies
978-0-7645-5296-0

Buddhism For Dummies,
2nd Edition
978-1-118-02379-2

Catholicism For Dummies,
2nd Edition
978-1-118-07778-8

Self-Help & Relationships

Beating Sugar Addiction
For Dummies
978-1-118-54645-1

Meditation For Dummies,
3rd Edition
978-1-118-29144-3

Seniors

Laptops For Seniors
For Dummies, 3rd Edition
978-1-118-71105-7

Computers For Seniors
For Dummies, 3rd Edition
978-1-118-11553-4

iPad For Seniors
For Dummies, 6th Edition
978-1-118-72826-0

Social Security
For Dummies
978-1-118-20573-0

Smartphones & Tablets

Android Phones
For Dummies, 2nd Edition
978-1-118-72030-1

Nexus Tablets
For Dummies
978-1-118-77243-0

Samsung Galaxy S 4
For Dummies
978-1-118-64222-1

Samsung Galaxy Tabs
For Dummies
978-1-118-77294-2

Test Prep

ACT For Dummies,
5th Edition
978-1-118-01259-8

ASVAB For Dummies,
3rd Edition
978-0-470-63760-9

GRE For Dummies,
7th Edition
978-0-470-88921-3

Officer Candidate Tests
For Dummies
978-0-470-59876-4

Physician's Assistant Exam
For Dummies
978-1-118-11556-5

Series 7 Exam For Dummies
978-0-470-09932-2

Windows 8

Windows 8.1 All-in-One
For Dummies
978-1-118-82087-2

Windows 8.1 For Dummies
978-1-118-82121-3

Windows 8.1 For Dummies
Book + DVD Bundle
978-1-118-82107-7

Available in print and e-book formats.

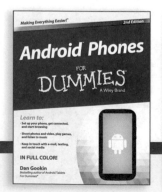

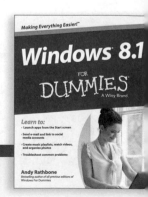

Available wherever books are sold. **For more information or to order direct visit www.dummies.com**

Take Dummies with you everywhere you go!

Whether you are excited about e-books, want more from the web, must have your mobile apps, or are swept up in social media, Dummies makes everything easier.

Visit Us

bit.ly/JE0O

Like Us

on.fb.me/1f1ThNu

Follow Us

bit.ly/ZDytkR

Watch Us

bit.ly/gbOQHn

Join Us
d.in/1gurkMm

Pin Us

bit.ly/16caOLd

Circle Us

bit.ly/1aQTuDQ

Shop Us

bit.ly/4dEp9

Leverage the Power

For Dummies is the global leader in the reference category and one of the most trusted and highly regarded brands in the world. No longer just focused on books, customers now have access to the For Dummies content they need in the format they want. Let us help you develop a solution that will fit your brand and help you connect with your customers.

Advertising & Sponsorships

Connect with an engaged audience on a powerful multimedia site, and position your message alongside expert how-to content.

Targeted ads • Video • Email marketing • Microsites • Sweepstakes sponsorship

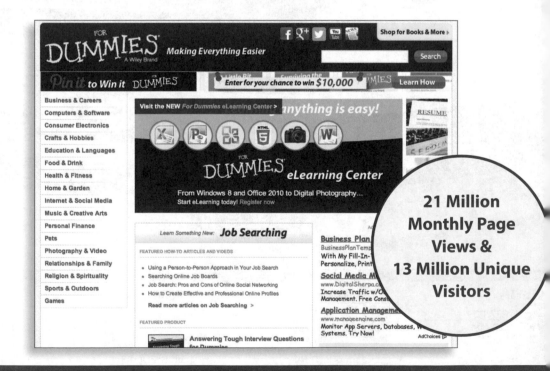

21 Million Monthly Page Views & 13 Million Unique Visitors

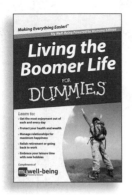

Dummies products make life easie

- DIY
- Consumer Electronics
- Crafts

- Software
- Cookware
- Hobbies

- Videos
- Music
- Games
- and More!

For more information, go to **Dummies.com** and search the store by category.

FOR
DUMMIE
A Wiley B

Make your **smartwatch** work for you

The Gear S2 is a useful mobile device, and it offers an easy way to get information quickly – at the glance of your wrist. However, if you're like most people, getting used to new technology can be a bit intimidating. Luckily, this book provides easy-to-follow guidance you can count on to make it a breeze. In no time, you'll have your new Samsung Gear S2 smartwatch wrapped around your finger—as well as your wrist!

Inside...

- Perform the initial setup
- Charge the Gear S2
- Change wrist straps
- Personalize the settings
- Add and update apps
- Stylize the face
- Use the Phone app
- Play music
- Track your activities

Eric Butow has written 30 books, most recently *Blogging to Drive Business, Second Edition* and *Google Glass For Dummies*. Eric also developed and taught networking, computing, and usability courses for Ed2Go, Virtual Training Company, California State University – Sacramento, and Udemy.

Go to Dummies.com®

for videos, step-by-step examples, how-to articles, or to shop!

Computers/Hardware/Mobile Devices
$29.99 USA / $35.99 CAN / £21.99 UK

ISBN 978-1-119-27998-3
52999

for
dummies®
A Wiley Brand